With Chennault in China
A Flying Tiger's Diary

With Chennault in China
A Flying Tiger's Diary

Robert Moody Smith

(Assisted by Philip D. Smith)

Schiffer Military/Aviation History
Atglen, PA

ACKNOWLEDGMENTS

The cooperation and assistance from the members of the American Volunteer Group and other friends is sincerely appreciated. Those who contributed so graciously include William E. Schaper, Lt. Col. Donald L. Rodewald, John R. Rossi, Col. John M. Williams, Walter Dolan and Walter Pentecost.

Cover artwork by Steve Ferguson, Colorado Springs, CO.
ABOVE THE RIVER OF LIFE—In the desperate days of early 1942, an obsolete RAF air defense accompanied by the A.V.G. (American Volunteer Group) "Flying Tigers" flew some of the most dramtic aerial engagements of the Second World War. Illustrated is the A.V.G. 1st Sqn. Ldr. Bob Neale two miles above the broad muddy delta of Burma's Irrawaddy River rolling his P-40 #23 into an escape dive against the Japanese Type 97 army fighters executing the final assault upon the British stronghold at Rangoon. Despite the desperate circumstances, Neale personally prevailed in the failed venture to emerge as the highest scoring interceptor pilot of the campaign with 15.5 confirmed aerial victories.

The Allied defense of Rangoon, Burma, versus the superior Japanese Imperial Army land and air forces at the onset of the war ranks as one of the most hopeless and heroic in history. With their supply routes cut and no expectation of reinforcements, A.V.G. commander Claire Chennault desperately shuttled his three Tomahawk squadrons in and out of the air battle while holding his landing fields until the last possible moment. The crescendo came on February 25th with the Allied air defense reduced to eight RAF Hurricanes and eleven P-40s of Neale's "Adam and Eve" First Pursuit Squadron. In their final interception at the odds of six to one, they fought across the breadth of the Irawaddy River delta peninsula, slashing into the enemy bomber formations with their superior diving speeds and heavy fire-power. That day, twenty-five enemy aircraft fell with the loss of only one Hurricane, but the feat was in vain. Withing the next five days, the A.V.G. withdrew to Magwe in the north as the last Hurricanes were lost in action. Rangoon fell on March 5th and Chennault's men eventually retreated into southern China.

Book Design by Ian Robertson.
Copyright © 1997 by Robert M. Smith.
Library of Congress Catalog Number: 97-65067

Printed in the United States of America.
ISBN: 0-7643-0287-6

We are interested in hearing from authors with book ideas on related topics.

Published by Schiffer Publishing Ltd.
4880 Lower Valley Road
Atglen, PA 19310
Phone: (610) 593-1777
FAX: (610) 593-2002
E-mail: Schifferbk@aol.com
Please write for a free catalog.
This book may be purchased from the publisher.
Please include $2.95 postage.
Try your bookstore first.

Contents

FOREWORD

The prime motivation for writing this book was a letter I received from General Claire Lee Chennault in March, 1958, shortly before he died. He wrote: "Sometime if you have an opportunity, I wish you would write me a kind of outline story or history of our radio network. You know I was so busy with so many things all during the life of the AVG, that it is hard for me to recall details now. I may write a book eventually and I certainly would like to include the story of our communications net, which was far superior to anything of its kind anywhere else in the world."

I sent General Chennault some material that I had extracted from my diary. In April, 1958, I received a thank you letter in which he stated: "I certainly was pleased to receive your letter and the manuscript. As you know, the things you wrote in your diary are now history and I think that your complete diary, with a little polishing, would be a very interesting historical book.

"I have always stated and felt that the network set up by the AVG had no superior anywhere in the world and that, as a matter of fact, there was no precedent for such a communications and air-ground control net in all of history. I have also believed that if I had been acquainted with the plan for landing Doolittle's B-25s in China, we could have put one station in East China with ground to-air-communications and a small homing beacon that would have enabled the majority of Doolittle's planes to land safely. There is a field in East China designed and constructed for this purpose but unfortunately I was not taken in on the secret and no communications for group-to-air were established.

"I will always recall with gratitude the fine service you radiomen gave me because the very success of the operations always depended on our communications."

Therefore, this book is for the General.

1

The Flying Tiger Story

Millions of Americans have heard of the Flying Tigers, but we who were part of that World War II organization in China and Burma didn't learn that the news media were calling us that until the spring of 1942, many months after our American Volunteer Group arrived in the Far East.

When I was told at my radio station at Chenyi in China's Yunnan Province that we were known in China, America and even Europe as the Flying Tigers, I thought it sounded silly, because tigers can't fly. Until the Japanese Air Force attacked Pearl Harbor on December 7, 1941 (it was December 8 to us in Burma), we were officially designated as the "First American Volunteer Group," for a second and a third group were planned but never organized.

After the United States declared war on Japan on December 8, 1941, the "first" was dropped, and we were usually called the "AVG." The first mention of the Flying Tiger name in the *New York Times* was on March 24, 1942, in a story by Spencer Moosa, an Associated Press correspondent. He said that this nickname came out of a Chinese newspaper that referred to us as *fei-hu* (flying tigers). In Chinese mythology the tiger outranks other animals and is often depicted as showing power and authority.

Whatever we were called at home and abroad during the war and afterwards, many books and hundreds of articles have been written about us. The AVG were the first to defeat the Japanese military forces in the China-Burma-India theater of the war. We were the only group having victories in the CBI area when disaster followed disaster for Allied armies all over the Far East.

But not so well known is how our commanding officer, Claire Lee Chennault, developed an extensive radio, telegraph and telephone network that aided our victories over the previously all-powerful Japanese Air Force. As a radioman, it was my job to work closely with the Chinese air raid warning net and relay information to our net control station and planes in the air.

Chennault, who lived from 1893 to 1958, was a rebel whose ideas on the use of air power often differed with orthodox methods of military schools before the war. This disagreement was part of acrimonious controversies that began after World War I over the selection and deployment of aircraft in winning battles.

Army generals originally thought of aviation as a tool for aiding ground troops to defeat enemy units. Navy admirals considered the airplane as a scouting mechanism to help sink opposing fleets. They both denied that air power could be decisive in wars.

In 1925 General William "Billy" Mitchell was court- martialed and sentenced to five years' suspension from service because he criticized the decreasing emphasis on aviation by the United States War and Navy Departments. He resigned from the Army in 1926 to present a series of lectures advocating reform in American aviation practices. But it was not until World War II that his recommendations for a strong air force were incorporated into official military policy.

By 1930, however, the standard theory of aerial warfare was that bombers could succeed in the face of enemy fighters and needed no fighter protection. The main achievement of the airplane in the first world war was overlooked or ignored: fighter aircraft demonstrated that they could devastate unescorted bombers.

In the United States the fighter plane seemed outmoded. Because of this attitude, pre-World War II bombers of the old Army Air Corps were built to fly faster with more firepower than the fighters of those years. It was a classic case of "getting the cart before the horse"—of mixing up priorities in preparing for future conflicts.

But American military officers had a few rebels who dared to denounce this misguided concept. They included Mitchell and Chennault, then an instructor in the Air Corps Tactical School at Maxwell Field, Alabama, in the 1930's. Chennault challenged traditional fighter doctrine in a mimeographed textbook, originally entitled *The Role of Defensive Pursuit*. He did not agree with the then-accepted viewpoint that "bombardment, once in the air, cannot be stopped."

Chennault countered this dogma with an argument against theorists who maintained that bombers were invincible, that they overlooked "the ancient principle that 'for every new weapon there is an effective counter weapon.' The pursuit plane was this antidote," he declared, for, if used effectively, it could intercept and destroy oncoming bombers.

Of course, later in World War II this was proved innumerable times in both Asia and Europe—victory in the air depended on the correct employment of fighter planes. Chennault was ahead of his time, however. His textbook contained the strategy and tactics that our Flying Tiger pilots used with so much success in Burma and China.

The book became the basic text for our AVG pilots. Successful air defense, Chennault wrote, required three essentials: detection, then interception, and finally destruction or "repulse of the invaders." His method is somewhat analogous to Aron Nimzovich's famous system for playing chess: restrict, blockade, destroy.

Chennault's text stressed that defending pursuit planes could intercept attacking bombers before they reached their targets if furnished timely information and if the interception area had enough depth to provide for necessary time factors.

He also maintained that bombers, flying far into hostile territory, must have supporting fighter protection to avoid catastrophic losses or complete failure of their assigned tasks. He said that long-range fighters must be developed with adequate armament and the dual ability of accompanying bombing missions and strafing enemy ground troops and bases.

Another important point of his book was his advocacy of two fighter pilots being trained to go into combat in pairs rather than in individual pursuit or large group action. He based his theory on the practice of the German World War I fighter plane aces, Baron Manfred von Richtofen and Oswald von Boelcke.

Our AVG pilots soon discovered that flying in pairs was much more flexible and gave them the freedom to watch for enemy planes. The old three plane formation was very restrictive since they had to spend much time keeping an eye on the other ships in the three unit formation to avoid collision. It was difficult to turn with three fighters in a formation, for the outside ship had to speed up to maintain the correct position. In a three plane group the pilots were continually increasing and decreasing their speed. In a two plane formation the wing man could move from the right to the left of the flight leader and back again and still maintain the two ship element. In actual combat or in an attack on a bomber formation, the wing man would drop back and not attempt to maintain close contact.

Bomber formations containing many planes flying in three ship elements have little capacity for maneuver and are "sitting ducks" for determined fighters. If they have no fighter protection, they are particularly vulnerable.

Chennault studied records of aerial aviation in Europe during that conflict and found that many of the concepts that he had independently developed in Hawaii while with the U.S. Air Corps had been invented earlier by the Germans. Von Boelcke was "the real father of fighter tactics," according to Chennault, who wrote in his autobiography that the German ace discovered that "two planes could be maneuvered to fight together as a team, and he grasped the tremendous tactical implications of his discovery." It had been a military axiom that the difference between the firepower of two opposing forces is not the difference in the number of fire units but the square of the difference of this number. Chennault declared that this meant that von Boelcke's two-plane element enjoyed odds of four to one, not merely two to one.

A crucial part of Chennault's technique and one that he emphasized in his text was the question: how could detection be achieved? His answer was by a network of ground reporting stations, hopefully aided by aerial pickets who could track the bombers during their attacks and retreats. He wanted pursuit planes to stay on the ground until an operations center had mathematically calculated a probable point of interception.

While defensive aircraft hurried toward this point, a radio operator of the operations center could give their pilots data he was getting from ground observers. This would permit the flight to adjust its course to find the enemy craft before they could arrive at their planned targets.

When Chennault first wrote down his prophetic advice for the next world war, neither the ability to supply this information nor the ground control services existed. But he developed and proved his ideas while still an Air Corps officer of the United States. He demonstrated with other fliers how efficient well-directed team play could be in fighter squadrons if they had effective communications and intelligence.

Yet the generals at this time in the early 1930s ignored or denigrated his plea for a radical change in airpower strategy. After failing in attempts to convert him to more accepted procedures as a student and an instructor in the tactical school, in 1937 the military brass retired Captain Chennault at the age of 47 as physically unqualified for flying assignments because he was partially deaf and had chronic bronchitis.

While in the Barksdale Field, Louisiana, hospital, he received a letter from Roy Holbrook, a former Air Corps pilot with Chennault and then a military adviser for the Chinese government. Holbrook wrote Chennault that Madame Chiang Kai-shek wanted him to spend three months making an inspection of the Chinese Air Force. Chennault accepted and went to China.

After he got to Shanghai in the spring of 1937, Chennault found that China and Japan had a temporary truce in their long war since Japan's army first invaded part of China in 1931. But new Sino-Japanese fighting started within weeks after he arrived in Shanghai. Soon he had the job of supervising an air force made up of Chinese pilots and foreign mercenaries as well as training fliers. Chennault developed a new night fighting technique and promoted the establishment of a large radio and telephone network to warn of attacking Japanese bombers. He won the respect of both Generalissimo Chiang Kai-shek and his wife.

With help from the Russian Air Force and other foreign pilots, the Chinese Air Force, using Colonel Chennault's advice, scored some surprising victories against the Japanese. But in spite of these early triumphs, the invaders gradually secured control of North China, capturing Nanking and Hankow and forcing Chiang to move his capital inland to Chungking. Continual fighting had all but destroyed the Chinese Air Force that Chennault had been building since 1937.

Madame Chiang, assigned by her husband to oversee his air force, then dusted off an old idea that had first been considered when the Japanese invaded Manchuria in 1932—foreign aviators would be employed not to be instructors but to fight for China. The United States would be asked to provide late model airplanes.

Although Chennault originally opposed the scheme, he and Major General Mao Pang-Tzo, director of the Chinese Air Force's Operations Division, met with Chiang in Chungking in October, 1940, to plan how China might build a new air force to counter the ever-attacking Japanese. Mao and Chennault were then sent to the United States to buy modern fighter planes and recruit experienced American pilots and ground crews.

In Washington, D.C., on November 25, 1940, they presented Chiang's request to the President's Liaison Committee, a civilian agency coordinating foreign arms purchases in the United States. The Chinese government asked that it be permitted to buy 660 planes, including 500 for combat, 150 for training and ten transports. It also wanted to purchase enough technical equipment to help build fourteen major airfields and 122 landing strips and to supply them with sufficient ammunition and ordnance for one year's operation.

The Chinese actually built the airfields with hand labor. They needed radios, landing lights, engines, steam rollers and similar gear. The Generalissimo also requested permission to recruit volunteers in the United States to fly, service the aircraft and teach Chinese aviators to fly them.

Some American government officials found these proposals unbelievable because of the urgent necessity of supplying Great Britain with aircraft and other equipment and supplies. Great Britain needed this equipment so that she could withstand German assaults during the Battle of Britain between the air forces of the Nazis and the British. American plane production was low at this time—not until 1943 or 1944 did American factories produce 50,000 aircraft a year. Another impediment to the Chinese mission was the rapid expansion of the United States military forces then underway. So, military leaders refused to consider Chiang's appeals for help.

All was not lost, however. Chennault, Mao and Dr. T.V. Soong, Chinese ambassador to the United States, found two supporters for their mission among Franklin D. Roosevelt's top advisors in the White House—Thomas Corcoran and Lauchlin Currie. Soon two members of FDR's cabinet also began to argue that China must get important aid for its air force from America. They were Frank Knox, Secretary of the Navy, and Henry Morgenthau, Secretary of the Treasury. The four Americans and Soong talked President Roosevelt into favoring the project.

It now may be forgotten that the United States was very pacifistic at this time. As is true today, its people didn't like foreign wars. But the Chinese proposal was the type that Roosevelt would like as a "short of war" move. Therefore, after the Roosevelt government became interested in the defense of the Burma Road against the Japanese Army, Chennault and Mao's assignment became feasible. With White House approval they began to visit aircraft plants to hunt for available planes.

Because the Royal Air Force had top priority in purchasing American planes and also because of the expansion of the air units of the American Army and Navy, orders had been placed with manufacturers for military aircraft that far exceeded their capacity to deliver. The possibility of obtaining 660 planes was very remote.

With the assistance of Burdette Wright, vice-president of the Curtiss-Wright Aircraft Corporation, and its agent in China, William D. Pawley, Soong's purchasing agents in the United Stated found 100 P-40Bs (H-81-A-2 by Curtiss-Wright or British nomenclature). They originally had been scheduled for lend-lease to Sweden, but with the fall of France in 1940 the British took over the allotment. The RAF was promised a more advanced model of the P-40 and gave up its priority so Chennault and Mao could obtain their aircraft for China.

The P-40s were to be paid for from loans totaling $150 million that Soong negotiated for China from the United States. This was possible when Congress included Chiang's government in its lend-lease legislation. Later we discovered that the planes were not equipped with radios, gunsights, bomb racks or provisions for attaching auxiliary fuel tanks to the wings or bellies of the P-40s to increase their range. A great deal of our effort in training and combat in Burma and China was spent on makeshift attempts to overcome these shortcomings.

By February, 1941, the P-40s were on the docks of New York harbor awaiting shipment to Rangoon, Burma. Unfortunately, there was a delay of about two months caused by some legal wranglings among Pawley, Curtiss-Wright and Chinese representatives in the United States. Pawley demanded, through his contract with the aircraft manufacturer, a commission of $450,000, which was ten percent of the purchase price for the stripped-down planes. Finally, he got $250,000 and the planes were shipped to Burma on a slow Norwegian ship. The cautious Norwegian captain undertook slow, evasive maneuvers to avoid Japanese and German submarines so the ship arrived thirty days overdue. One of the P-40s was lost overboard in Rangoon harbor while being unloaded.

It was more difficult to get Chennault's fliers and support crew than it was to secure the aircraft. The only places to find qualified pilots and other experienced men were the Army Air Corps, the Naval Air Service and the Marine Aviation Wing. But all of them were expanding, and they needed all their officers and enlisted men.

After continual refusals by the generals and admirals commanding these services to allow Chennault's recruiters to sign up their personnel, Chennault turned to Secretary Morgenthau once more. With additional help from Thomas Corcoran, President Roosevelt issued a direct order to all services to permit recruiters on all air bases and allow interested pilots and ground crews to sign contracts for service in the Far East. At last the American Volunteer Group became possible. Since American foreign policy was then still appeasing the Japanese government, the Central Aircraft Manufacturing Company and China Defense Supplies were used as intermediaries.

Eventually 109 pilots and 190 enlisted men were given honorable discharges from the American military services to accept one year contracts with CAMCO. Some AVG personnel were recruited in the Orient. Chennault brought to Burma his group of former Army, Navy and Marine Corps officers and supporting ground crews, as well as three nurses, a chaplain and other new CAMCO employees.

In addition to pilots, Chennault recruited a large contingent of enlisted men from the American military forces. They included line chiefs, mechanics, armorers, radio operators and repairmen (including me), mess sergeants, propeller specialists, parachute riggers, photographers, finance paymasters and medical orderlies.

Today Chennault's organization of this American Volunteer Group and its successes are part of aviation history. After July 4, 1942, some of the Flying Tigers joined the China Air Task Force of the U.S. Air Force under Chennault's command on that date or accepted temporary duty with the CATF until new personnel could be trained to replace most of the AVG pilots and ground crew who returned to the United States. Most of them entered the American military services or support groups. Later many of them, including me, returned to China. I came back with the Army Airways Communications System and was the first commanding officer of the 159th AACS Squadron. The task force was succeeded by the Fourteenth Air Force under Major General Chennault in March, 1943.

Chennault's fighter tactics have now been accepted as models. With a limited number of poorly equipped and antiquated aircraft, the AVG's achievements are unsurpassed in the history of World War II air power. In no other area of that worldwide conflict was so much destruction of enemy forces attained with such limited means.

Because they did not have gun cameras which were used later in the war to confirm enemy aircraft losses, Chennault's fliers were not always sure of how many Japanese planes they shot down. Even today different books on the AVG have conflicting statistics. Official records of the Chinese Air Force state that from the time when the Flying Tigers started their air combat on December 20, 1941, until the AVG was merged into the U.S. Army Tenth Air Force and reorganized as the Twenty-Third Fighter Group on July 4, 1942, "it had participated in one hundred two air campaigns and launched five hundred twelve sorties with two hundred sixty eight Japanese planes destroyed, forty damaged, fifty-six probably shot down and eight probably destroyed."

Official statistics of the AVG kept by Mrs. Olga Greenlaw, the wife of Chennault's first executive officer, credit the group with destroying 299 Japanese planes—more than the confirmed kills that the Chinese government paid for at $500 per aircraft. Her records state that the Tiger pilots possibly shot down 153 additional planes and ruined 200 more on the ground. Twenty-three Flying Tigers were killed in action or as a result of accidents in Burma and China.

Thirty-three of the AVG fliers became aces for shooting down five or more enemy aircraft, although some of them did not achieve this mark until later when they were with the task force or the Fourteenth Air Force. Some of the original Flying Tigers acquired additional fame in World War II in other theaters of combat. Two of them won Congressional Medals of Honor: Colonel Gregory "Pappy" Boyington, a leader of the Marine Corps' Black Sheep squadron in the South Pacific, and General Jim Howard, who, with the Air Force in Europe again became an ace.

For about $8 million—to buy and equip the air planes, including some P-40Es as replacements—and approximately $3 million to recruit and operate the original AVG group until its official end, China bought a number of important victories.

Our group cleared the northern end of the Burma Road of Japanese bomber attacks and then, with limited aid from the British Royal Air Force, kept the Japanese Army from capturing Rangoon for two and a half months while thousands of tōns of much-needed war supplies were being hurried up that road to China. We were finally forced out of Rangoon by advancing Japanese ground troops, since British resistance on the Malay Peninsula and in Burma was limited. Another AVG accomplishment after the Japanese captured most of Burma was to impede an enemy offensive into Southern China in the Salween Gorge on the famous Burma Road. The Tigers also drove Japanese planes from the much-attacked Hunan and Kwangi Provinces and provided Chungking with its first bomb-free summer in four years.

Basic to these brilliant achievements was Chennault's development of a top-notch communications system. The Chinese air-warning net was recognized as the best in the world until radar was introduced. This procedure originated from Chennault's writings in the 1930s that argued that the problem of pursuit plane interception could be stated in a mathematical formula using speed, altitude and rate of climb of approaching enemy aircraft. This would permit pursuit aircraft to intercept them before they reached their intended targets.

Chennault believed that with this continuous information, his commanders could launch their fighters into the air at the right time and place to intercept and defeat bombers before they arrived at their planned points of attack.

By 1938 the Japanese military juggernaut had captured most of China that was worth taking. This overwhelming force destroyed or controlled China's main railroads and had secured the Yangtze and Yellow Rivers, thereby controlling China's rice fields. The Japanese had taken over ninety-five percent of China's industry, seized major seaports and defeated the Chinese armed forces. But remnants of that "lost" army struggled on into 1941, and the Chinese National Government precariously survived in Chungking on top of a mountain near one of the loops of the Yangtze. China was isolated.

The Japanese did not stop with China. They occupied most of Indochina and compelled the British to close the Burma Road for three months. The Burma Road was the final supply line to China from Rangoon. It started at the railhead at Lashio in North Burma and wound about 700 tortuous miles across mountain ranges to Kunming in China's Yunnan Province. The enemy's occupation of Hanoi cut off the railroad to Kunming that had been built by the French conquerors of Indochina. After Hong Kong was captured by the Japanese in December, 1941, the last air route between the China coast and the National Government of Chiang Kai-shek in Chungking was lost.

In the fall of 1941 the United States forced Britain to reopen the Burma Road, and the first American aid began to arrive in southwest China. A few thousand tons per day was a small percentage of what was required by the surviving Chinese government, its army and people. Much of the American supplies for China never arrived, but this was better than nothing. It had to go from the port of Rangoon to Kunming across the Burma Road, built by thousands of Chinese coolies.

It was a long and expensive line of communication, but it was worth any price to keep open. Before the Burma Road reopened, Chennault had warned the Chinese High Command that it would be a main target for Japanese bombers. He started to plan the aerial defense of this all-important supply link to what survived of China.

He was aware that the Japanese had no fighter planes with sufficient range to escort bombers from Indochinese bases to Burma Road targets. Therefore, he hoped to develop a defensive pursuit group of 100 to 200 fighter planes that could attack enemy squadrons. He wanted to have an air umbrella of fighters over important points on the Burma Road in both Burma and China so that truck convoys could move up the mountain passes safely. When Japanese bombers appeared in this region, Chennault could use his warning net to plan his counterattack.

His plans were theoretical until the first part of 1941, when the United States accepted responsibility for sending the lend-lease supplies to China. Then the Flying Tigers became a reality. The Central Aircraft Manufacturing Company had been organized by William Pawley and had an assembly plant in China at Loiwing and offices in New York, Hong Kong and Rangoon. To try to prevent American government embarrassment with the military regime of Japan, CAMCO was authorized to employ about a hundred American pilots and some two hundred ground personnel under a one year contract to "operate, service and manufacture aircraft in China." The contracts provided for pilots to earn between $600 and $750 a month, while ground personnel's pay ranged originally from $150 to $350 per month. Some line or crew chiefs were raised to $400 later in China or Burma. Fliers also were to receive $500 for each enemy plane destroyed if these kills were confirmed.

The beginning of the assembly of the P-40s at Rangoon in the summer of 1941. The crated plane is being removed from the flatbed truck by coolies.

Since the commanders of the American military services would not allow staff officers to join the Flying Tigers in 1941, Chennault had to choose his group staff from men not in the armed forces or already in China. A first group of thirty AVG personnel left San Francisco on an army transport for the Philippines and arrived in Rangoon on another ship in July, 1941. A second group of us, totaling 123, left San Francisco on July 10 of that year on a Dutch ship, the Jaeqersfontein. Three other Dutch ships of the Java-Pacific Line brought the rest of the group to Burma.

Our passports listed us as students, vaudeville artists, school teachers, musicians, salesmen, bank employees and, in my case, a radio announcer, since I had worked in that capacity at KFXJ for two years in Grand Junction, Colorado. After the second contingent got to Rangoon in late July, the others did not arrive until August or September.

Walter Pentecost, who had studied Allison engines at their Indianapolis factory while working for the North American Corporation, was assigned to supervise the assembling of our P-40s, which had been shipped in crates. He was handicapped by inadequate tools and equipment, unskilled Burmese workers and the approach of the rainy season in Rangoon. The resulting delays kept the first assembled planes from reaching our training base at Toungoo until August, 1941.

Chennault then pressured CAMCO to send several Chinese and American mechanics from its Loiwing plant to the P-40 assembly plant at the Mingaladon airfield near Rangoon. A sheltered factory was constructed to escape the monsoon. The trained technicians helped Pentecost complete twenty-two P-40s in August, twenty-one in September, twenty-nine in October and the final twenty-seven in November.

After short test flights the planes were flown to Toungoo's Kyedaw airdrome in Burma, where ground crewmen installed machine guns and homemade gunsights, radios and oxygen equipment. Chennault explained that the P-40s were not an ideal plane, for most of them were fitted with British .303 caliber wing machine guns instead of American .30 caliber guns.

The problem of getting this British-type ammunition for these guns was one of our biggest headaches in Burma. We also received planes without radios, since China Defense Supplies was unable to buy military radio equipment. It had to substitute Piper Cub sport-plane radio sets, providing us with another hazard in our operations, because they could not stand up in continual combat and often failed at embarrassing times. I helped install the radio equipment.

The planes had also arrived in Burma without even spare spark plugs, so spare parts were obtained all over Southeast Asia from Karachi to Manila. Chennault was pessimistic about getting replacements for his original ninety-nine planes. He told

Towing a P-40 to the flying base for test flights and final acceptance. This towing covered a distance of one mile and was done by a truck and rope. No tow bars were available.

P-40s being assembled at Rangoon. The sun sheds were built to protect the mechanics from the hot Burma sun and tropical rain.

his supply officer, C.B. "Skip" Adair, "We can't last fifteen days in China without more planes and more supplies."

We did eventually get some more meager equipment, supplies and spare parts and some P-40s in the spring of 1942. But all of them were always inadequate for the monumental tasks assigned to our pilots. Our Tomahawks were obsolete by most World War II standards. The chief of the U.S. Army Air Force, General Henry B. Arnold, considered them to be nothing better than trainers.

Final plane assembly building at Rangoon.

Walter Pentecost, who was in charge of the P-40 assembly operation, in front of a local sign that was "improved" by some Californians. A copy of this picture was given to the Los Angeles Chamber of Commerce.

When the Tigers went into action against the Japanese (starting in the defense of Rangoon in late December of 1941), the Curtiss-Wright plant in Buffalo was manufacturing the advanced P-40Es and P-40Fs, known as the Kittyhawk and the Warhawk. The Tomahawk was a low-wing, single-seater monoplane with a twelve-cylinder liquid-cooled Allison engine and 1,150 horsepower. Equipped with six machine guns for combat, the P-40B had an actual top speed of 300 miles an hour at 10,000 feet and fifteen miles less than that at 20,000 feet, although the factory claimed faster operating speeds.

Chennault admitted that he was not keen on the P-40B originally, because of the vulnerability of its liquid-cooled engine in combat. He also thought it might be too heavy and too slow to fight the fast-climbing Nates and Zeros of the Japanese Air Forces.

The AVG called all Japanese fighter planes Zeros, although there were not many of them in action against us. The Nate—the Nakajima Ki-27 fighter plane—was the backbone of the Japanese Air Force for several years of the war in China after its introduction in 1938. Like most Japanese fighters, it lacked sufficient armor for pilot protection but was very maneuverable.

The famous Zero—the Mitsubishi A6M—was known by this appellation because the Imperial Japanese Navy had designated it as the Model O carrier fighter. After its appearance in 1939 it was considered a dangerous weapon in the hands of a competent pilot.

In Japanese planes the need to reduce weight forced their designers to dispense with self-sealing integral fuel cells and armor protection for fliers. As a result, the enemy aircraft, particularly the Zeros, could "turn on a dime," as Chennault put it, and were heavily armed.

Since the Japanese Zeros were highly maneuverable and our P-40s were not, Chennault trained our pilots never to get into a dog fight with a Zero, for it would have meant death! Our pilots' goal in combat was to fly as high as possible, dive, make a pass at enemy planes in pairs while firing accurately, and then go back up to do all of this again. The diving speed of a P-40 was very fast, faster than a Zero's. Since the accepted dogma was individual dogfights between opposing aircraft, the Japanese designed their Zeros and other fighters to be the best dogfighters. They were—we could not defeat them on their own terms.

When our first AVG group was in Burma and China, opposing our pilots from bases in China, Indochina and Thailand were seventy Japanese Air Force squadrons with 620 aircraft, of which about 340 were fighters. They later were reinforced

This was the last P-40 assembled at Rangoon. One hundred H81-A-2 aircraft were delivered to Burma, but one was lost in the bay. It was later retrieved and used for spare parts. Its wing was used later on P-8194.

Walter Pentecost in a P-40. This picture was taken at Loiwing after Rangoon was abandoned.

Pentecost with P-40 at Loiwing. He was preparing to taxi the plane to a revetment area.

The beginning of the Burma Road at Lashio. (From the Walter Pentecost collection.)

by 191 enemy planes from the Imperial Navy after our pilots cut the Japanese Army Air Force squadrons to pieces at a ratio of twelve kills for one of our planes lost.

Before Pearl Harbor, Chennault divided our P-40s into three squadrons of eighteen planes each. The first was known as Adam and Eves, and the others were called Panda Bears and Hell's Angels. The three outfits never had more than a total of fifty-five planes ready for combat.

Chennault had planned to train us in then-neutral Burma when we first arrived from the United States to avoid Japanese attacks before we were prepared to fight. Since the airfield at Kunming was not ready, the Chinese government arranged with the RAF to use its Toungoo base. After the United States entered the war, Chennault realized that we could not remain at Toungoo without risking destruction by enemy bombers, since we were not protected by an air raid warning net.

He then planned to move our three squadrons to Kunming, the Yunnan capital, where the Chinese had built a 7,000 foot runway. From this air base, the AVG could protect China's part of the Burma Road. But the British wanted the group to operate from Mingladon to defend the Burma end of China's lifeline and Rangoon. Chiang

Building an airfield in China. The large stone rollers were made by local craftsmen and dragged up and down the runway by many coolies. In Chinese the word coolie means "bitter work."

settled this dispute by ordering Chennault to send one squadron to help the RAF protect Rangoon and to dispatch the other two to Kunming. The Hell's Angels assisted the British in defending Rangoon and were later replaced by the Panda Bears.

The rest of this story is told by my diary as one of the ground crew, a radioman. I was with the second ship to Rangoon that left San Francisco in July, 1941 (the *Jaegersfontein*), and with the AVG evacuation over the Burma Road to Kunming the following December.

2

The Diary

June 26, 1941. *I was honorably discharged today from the 20th Pursuit Group, Army Air Force, "for the convenience of the government." Just a week ago I signed a contract with the Central Aircraft Manufacturing Company to go to China to join a group or squadron of fighter planes to protect the Burma Road. The contract is for one year after we get to China. I am to be paid $300 a month plus quarters and all transportation. A.A. Miller, who also is a radioman from Headquarters Squadron, has signed up, too. Jim Musick and Bill Schaper, both mechanics, are also joining us.*

I have always wanted to see more of the world and experience adventure with a big "A" ever since I read Richard Haliburton's The Royal Road To Romance. *I would have signed up for $100 a month.*

We have to report in San Francisco on July 5, so I will go to Los Angeles for a few more days to see the family. I will hitchhike to save money.

July 4, 1941. *I left Los Angeles today by train for San Francisco in order to be there on the fifth as required by my contract. I said good-bye to Mother, Lew and the Alhambra relatives who came down to Union Station to see me off. From the tears in the eyes of everyone, including my uncle, William Dutton, one would think that I was never coming back. Mother felt very badly; my brother Lewis was very much the man for his fifteen years. Philip, who is twenty-three, wasn't there, for he went to the mountains for the weekend.*

I met Jim Musick on the train in the club car. We drank beer and talked of what we would see and do in China. We were very happy about our salaries. Three hundred a month plus expenses sure beats the $84 I got as a sergeant air mechanic first class.

July 5, 1941. *Reported in at the Bellevue Hotel in San Francisco. It is filled with all of the CAMCO crowd. There are at least 100 of us here. Everyone is in holiday spirits. We have a bar in our room with an electric icebox which attracted visitors.*

July 6, 1941. *I saw Sylvia, Phil's girlfriend. We talked about China. Everyone in our group is trying to get the most out of 'Frisco for the last time.*

July 10. *We sailed from San Francisco westward on the* M.S. Jaegersfontein, *a ship of the Dutch V.N.S. (Java Pacific) line. On board are 122 Americans going to China, all signed up by the Central Aircraft Manufacturing Company, which we call CAMCO. Most of the army men come from the U.S. Air Corps' best pursuit groups, the 20th, the 1st and the 8th. The navy men come from all over the world, some from the secret warfare in the Atlantic. Bill Sykes, an ex-navy radioman, told of the sinking of a German submarine a few weeks ago by a U.S. destroyer. Everyone knows about the secret war except the American public.*

Played bridge with Musick, Hauser and Arvo Miller. The servants on the ship are Javanese, "boys" who wear colorful turbans and white coats. The service is excellent, but they don't speak Dutch, let alone English.

July 15. *Sighted the Hawaiian Islands this afternoon. We docked around 8:30 p.m. and went ashore at ten o'clock. The local port authorities were very efficient. Honolulu is full of sailors, for it's payday. The local "houses" had customers lined up, just like a butcher shop. The shore patrol was doing a fine business.*

July 16. *I bought some silk sport shirts and a few other things, soap, a pen, pencils and some notebooks. I bought two leis for a quarter each. The flowers were very fragrant. A Hawaiian woman with a shy, friendly smile sold them to us. When we sailed out of the harbor past Diamond Head, we tossed them over the rail. The tradition says that if they float back to the beach, one will return to "the beautiful isles of Hawaii."*

July 17. *At sea. Yesterday afternoon at one o'clock we left Honolulu and headed for the Philippines. We didn't know it, but we were following a United States cruiser. This morning we saw two cruisers on the horizon. They signaled and the* M.S. Jaegersfontein, *out of Batavia, Dutch East Indies, stood by. The warships pulled alongside. They are the* USS Salt Lake City *and the* USS Northhampton. *The latter dropped a boat and sent an officer, a Lieutenant Junior Grade, and two seamen aboard. The Lieutenant had a star on his shoulder indicating a staff officer. The seamen are signalmen and stayed on the* Jaegersfontein *after the officer left. They brought their sea bags and apparently will stay here for some days. The two ships are ahead now and we are following them.*

This would make headlines in the States. Lindberg and Wheeler would rant and rave. Two United States ships convoying one Dutch freighter! I guess the cargo on this ship must be valuable!

July 18. *We lost another half hour today, or rather we set our watches back a half hour. The weather is warmer, for we are going south and west. Our convoy is still with us. There are rumors aboard that there are two enemy raiders near here—either German or Japanese. I'll guess they are German.*

July 20. *Sunday. Church services were held in the music salon this morning. I played bridge instead of going. The* Northhampton *and the* Salt Lake City *are still ahead. We are sailing south and a little west, as we have been for four days. We are only going at about half-speed or ten knots. We made seventeen knots between San Francisco and Oahu. Yesterday we practiced several unusual maneuvers under orders of the admiral. No one knows why except our captain.*

Tomorrow we cross "the great dividing line," according to an announcement from the ship's purser. I expect that we'll all get initiated into the Royal Society of HIH Emperor Neptune. I'm taking a class in Chinese. The teacher is a Ph.D., Stephen P.Y. Pau, who is traveling third class on the ship. He is charging us each a dollar a lesson.

July 27. *Yesterday was July 25. We crossed the international dateline last night and thereby lost a day. Today is the third Sunday aboard. The cruisers are still ahead. We have not sighted land since Oahu. It rained last night, and it is cloudy and moist and cool for a change. The captain will not tell us our position, but I think we are thirteen degrees south of the equator and on the date line. This should put us near the Fiji Islands. Don't know what our next port will be, hopefully Manila as planned. We are to be paid there. Some of the men are running short of money—I have made a few small loans. Our credit is good at the bar, and we can charge our cigarettes. The pilots look so young; many are only about twenty-one years old. The ground crew are older by several years. I am twenty-six. I wonder how they will do in China.*

July 28. *Monday. It's rainy, cloudy and cool for a change. At night we are blacked out with all doors and port holes closed. It is uncomfortably hot in the bar and music salon. It's too hot to read, and the lights are too dim, anyway.*

We play bridge and drink rum collins. The nearest land is two miles down. We're twenty-two days out of Honolulu and still no hint of our next port. I'm beginning to doubt that we are going to the Philippines.

The ship rolls more now; things slide around on the tables. We would welcome a storm to break the monotony, but, as we are drawing our pay, we shouldn't mind too much.

The Dutch captain says the war should last five more years and then end with a general revolution. The radio news reports that Russia is holding the line, the Germans are blaming the weather, and that the Huns are sterilizing the men in occupied countries and breeding the women with pure Aryan stock.

July 30. *It is cool today. July in the southern hemisphere is wintertime and I imagine we are far enough south to notice the difference. I am not sure of our position, but I think it is near Australia. We are one hour ahead of eastern Australian time and have been for two days. We should change time again tonight. I finished reading R. H. Bruce Lockhart's* Return To Malaya. *I enjoyed it, for it tells quite a bit about the Dutch East Indies. I wonder if we will stop at Bali.*

Passage on this ship from San Francisco to Rangoon cost CAMCO $490 per man.

August 6. *We came through the Torres Straits on the third. We lost our two U.S. cruisers and picked up a Dutch gunboat, apparently a prearranged meeting. Rumor says that the reason we lost so much time was due to a mistake in Washington, for government officials thought that this ship could do but twelve knots instead of sixteen or more.*

A pilot was with the Dutch gunboat to show us through the straits. We dropped him at the western end of a large island. Although the islands were very barren and had few trees, I yearned to get off and stretch my legs. Those rough hills sticking out of the sea were very attractive after so many miles of monotonous ocean.

Cameras were turned in yesterday and all film confiscated. The Torres Straits are mined, and the channel is a military secret.

I heard on the radio that the USS Northhampton and Salt Lake City pulled into Brisbane, Australia, last night "on a routine training cruise."

We passed yesterday what I think is the Portuguese Island of Timor. I used to have stamps from there; I never thought that I would see it.

The Java boy is playing that tune on the chimes announcing that breakfast is ready.

August 7. *It is cloudy and warmer, and we are passing more islands. I think we are in the Flores Sea. There are quite a few sail boats and fishing smacks in the distance. One of them tried to come up to us to investigate, but we were too fast and left him in our wake.*

Dr. Richards and the medical staff aboard gave us a lecture this morning on tropical and venereal diseases. It appears that the Japanese bombers are the least of our worries. We have already received shots for cholera, smallpox, typhoid and yellow fever. We are to get shots for dysentery after we leave Manila. There are no vaccines for malaria or Rocky Mountain spotted fever and its cousins. These diseases are common where we are going.

We estimate that we are around 1,000 miles directly south of Manila. If we are to go there, we will have to turn north soon.

August 8. It is seven in the morning Manila time. We turned north sometime during the night, for the sun is coming up to the starboard. The island of Celebes is visible under the sun.

August 11. We landed at Singapore today, for the Dutch had orders to get rid of us here. The American consul had not heard of us. There are no rooms at any hotel and no transportation available to Rangoon. We may have to stay here for three months, according to one rumor. We hear that about thirty of our group were here a few weeks ago and did not endear themselves to the authorities. We went to town to see the sights while Charlie Mott, a pilot who is in charge of us, and the captain went to see the consul. Radiograms went out in all directions.

The British customs officers came aboard wearing sun helmets and white uniforms with white shorts. They wore white stockings that covered the calves of their legs, leaving the knees bare. They looked very military but strange to us, for the American army does not wear shorts in the United States. They looked like characters out of W. Somerset Maugham. Some of our guys whistled at them.

Singapore is filled with Chinese, Tamils, British soldiers and sailors, Sikhs and half a dozen other types that I cannot identify. Most of the natives are dirty. The dock hands wore single dirty towels draped around their heads, shirts of ancient and dubious manufacture and checkered tablecloths wrapped around their loins and tied in front. Many of them had fashionably long skirts that touched the ground. They also used them in lieu of handkerchiefs. Some of them omit the towel turban and wear hair that looks like it has never been cut.

Singapore is filled with one permeating odor that fills the streets, stores, cafes and theaters that is the result of open sewers—gutters that line the sidewalks. We crossed one canal that was so bad that we ran two blocks holding our noses to escape the worst of it. There are many other strange smells, all different, that seem to be attempting to subdue the rest.

Mothers and husbands here bargain for their daughters and wives. One Chinese wanted ten dollars for her fourteen-year-old daughter or five dollars American money. Several of the fellows, when they left in the morning, found the husbands sleeping on the floor or on a sofa outside the bedroom door.

Beer is 80¢ in local money, half that in ours. Good whiskey is only 20¢ American a shot. American cigarettes are about the same here as in the States. Watches are very cheap. One can buy a good fifteen-jewel Swiss movement for ten American dollars. Rents for Americans and other whites are very high. Wages for natives are low. Native carpenters get 19¢ to 25¢ an hour in the local currency. The exchange is roughly two to one in our favor.

Folding money here may mean ten Malay cents; there are also paper quarters and some small copper and silver coins.

Dishes are washed on the front sidewalks. Naked babies play in the streets. The Chinese eat their meals in their shops.

August 12. *We are not to leave the ship. The Jaegersfontein has been ordered to take us to Rangoon. Our trunks are being carried back on board. The American consul was violently opposed to having our group here for several weeks while waiting for another ship. Apparently he had trouble with the first group of our men and did not want 123 of us hanging around at loose ends. I am glad we got to go ashore last night to see the city.*

August 16. *Near Toungoo, Burma. We arrived at a Royal Air Force field for an indefinite stay. We are going to install radio equipment and guns in P-40s. The British call the field Kyedaw Airdrome.*

We were up at 5:30 this morning for coffee and then at nine we went on a lighter to the Rangoon docks. We had breakfast at the Silver Grill and were put on a special narrow gauge train that took us 200 miles north to Toungoo. We are in barracks built of teak and bamboo that have long narrow verandas on the western side. The beds have a sticker pasted on them saying "On His Majesty's Service." We sleep under mosquito nets. It is cloudy and raining. There are no American cigarettes, only British "Players" that taste like straw.

August 17. *Sunday. Everyone is either on his bed or drinking beer in the mess hall. Most of us went over to the hangar to look over the planes and equipment. Almost all of it is either in Rangoon or in China.*

August 18. *My first job is to remove all the radio wiring in the P-40s. The planes were built for the British and wired for their radio transmitters and receivers. But we do not have their equipment. Instead we have a radio transceiver RCA-7-H, which was built in the United States for Piper Cubs. I wonder how these radios will work in combat.*

LEFT: R.M. Smith at infantry R.O.T.C. summer camp at Fort Leavenworth, Kansas, in 1936. Notice the "wrap leggin's."

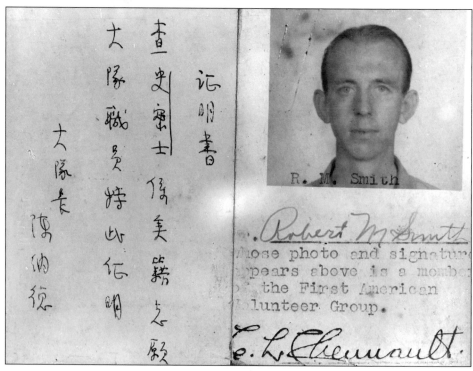

All members of the American Volunteer Group were issued these identification cards.

August 19. *Knocking out radio wiring is hot and difficult work. All I have is a very large screwdriver and a ball peen hammer to work with. I have to reach into the tail of the plane through a small door in the tail to get at the joints where the wiring is bolted to the plane.*

August 23. *I have been losing my breakfast about nine thirty every morning. The heat is terrible, humid and depressing. The tail of the P-40 is no ice box.*

August 26. *Colonel Chennault has changed our working hours since we cannot take the midday heat. We work early in the day and late in the evening as long as we can see what we are doing. For about three hours, from eleven until two, I lie on my bunk and sweat. I almost stepped on a krait last night; luckily my flashlight's beam caught him. I retreated warily, and he slithered off into the bush. Kraits are the most poisonous snake in the world; one can kill you in ninety seconds. I have learned to take all my clothes (except my shoes) to bed with me under the mosquito bar at night. If I do not, they are filled with strange bugs in the morning. I carefully knock all the bugs out of my shoes before I put them on.*

The AVG were visited by many British and American officers during the summer and fall of 1941. Visitors included Air Marshall Sir Robert Brook-Popham, British Commander-in-Chief of the Far East and Field Marshal Sir Archibald Wavell. Shown here is Air Vice Marshal Pulford being greeted by Chennault and Greenlaw at Toungoo.

The first thirty of the AVG to arrive in Toungoo. This picture was taken on the President Pierce. *Chaplain Paul Frillman was in charge of this group.*

R. M. Smith in Toungoo.

August 27. *The pilots are going to school. Many of the navy pilots have flown "big boats" or Catalinas and are not used to P-40s.*

September 8. *John D. Armstrong was killed today in a training accident. He is our first casualty. "Army" and Gil Bright were dogfighting near the air field when they collided. Bright bailed out and was not badly hurt. It was just the other day that I met "Army" down by the hangar. He had been riding his bicycle and stopped to talk to me. I discovered that he had gone to Kansas State, my own college, and had graduated in 1938. He had been the roommate of Thaine Engle, who was one of my best friends. Thaine and I worked together at KSAC, the college radio station where I wrote one or two half-hour dramatic shows a week for three years. I had never met "Army" at Kansas State. It is a sad day for us here.*

September 14. *Sunday. I went walking this morning in the brush with Jim Musick. He carried an air pistol, I a short stick. We headed north on a native path and found ourselves in a small clearing. It was a Buddhist village. Four or five small boys in their yellow robes came forward, very much interested in us and Jim's gun. One priest, about twenty years old, came out of one of the bamboo houses and smiled in a friendly fashion. But as I could not speak Burmese or he English, we made no contact. I had purchased a Burmese grammar published by the American Baptist Mission Press, but I have not made any progress beyond learning that "Burmese has three tones, the light, the checked and the heavy."*

Jim thought the priest was trying to invite us in to tea. I thought he was showing us the way out of the village. I was pointing and tried to ask for the road—that is the main one here, which is actually a part of the Burma Road. Later we found a boy who guided us back to our camp. We gave him an anna—about two cents.

Our hangar at Toungoo.

Burma is a land of rain, heat and rice paddies. There are many mountains and valleys green with fields and jungles. Elephants work in the teak forest, and coolies earn eight annas a day. It is a melting pot of the East. There are Indians, Burmese who look like the Chinese a bit, Karens, Kachins and other hill tribes, British representing the empire, Chinese fleeing from the Japanese and tall Sikhs with beards, gray eyes and turbans. Then add to this mixture us Americans. It is said that the East is hard to understand, but I am sure that the people here, including the British, find us more inexplicable. We are rich to them. One can realize that when we earn sixty-five times as much as the laborers here receive. Most of the heavy work is done by Indians who come here attracted by wages that are much better than in India. In the United States sixty five times the wage of unskilled labor would be riches. We make more than the officials here. One Anglo-Burman (part British, part Burmese) said that she always thought all Americans were like the local missionaries. Now she knows better with the army and navy representatives in town. We are rowdy, rich, objectionable, but friendly. But I doubt that we are understood, for how could we be when we ourselves are amazed at our fellows?

A Chinese merchant in Toungoo. He had this picture taken in Burmese native costume so that he could show his mother in China how the local people dressed.

September 23. *Max C. Hammer was killed yesterday in an accident near Rangoon. He got caught in a storm. The weather is terrible here for flying during the monsoon season.*

October 4. *It is a Burmese holiday, the "Feast of the Light." Walt Dolan and I went to a Burmese celebration in Toungoo in a truck that provides transportation for us*

Walter Dolan took this picture of hill tribe peoples on a trip into the mountains east of Toungoo. The brass rings around the necks of the women are a mark of status and beauty. This tribe is called the Padaung by the Burmese, but they call themselves the Keka-wngdu. They are a curiosity even to the Shan and local peoples.

in the evenings. It was a religious "pway" or play in English. We were the only white people there, and when the show started the Burmese found two chairs for us. Everyone else sat on the floor. Before the play began we sat cross-legged in the lobby of the temple and talked Burmese politics. We took off our shoes when we came in as a mark of respect, but it was okay to smoke and talk. One Burman, who spoke very good English, told us that many of the natives think the British have mortgaged Burma to the Americans and we are here to protect our interests. The show was colorful with odd music and bright costumes. We had to leave early to catch the last truck back to our base.

October 5. There are many Burma Road stories prevalent. Many of the hill tribes near the road on the China-Burma border are head hunters who kill their victim and bury the head under their house to provide good fortune for the family. White men's heads are prized, but a red head is the most valuable of all. The Japanese *bomb the road between the hours of eleven and three o'clock, so the trucks hole up for that period. Since convoys rarely travel at night due to bandits, travel is very slow.*

We have an English-speaking Karen from the hills working for us in the radio shack. He does odd jobs, stenciling shipping directions on boxes, packing supplies and taking care of our battery chargers. We are always charging batteries, since the radios we have are twelve volts and we have to tap one half of the planes' twenty-four volt batteries. He is an excellent worker. We pay him twenty-five rupees

An older hill tribe woman who seems to enjoy life.

a month or less than $10 in American currency. He cannot understand why we are worth thirty times as much as he is. I had trouble explaining it to him.

He had one pair of khaki shorts of which he was quite proud. However, he spilled battery acid on them and now he is wearing a Burmese long skirt.

Both Burmese men and women wear skirts. At first it was difficult to tell them apart, for both have small bones and similar stature. But I know how now. The women tie the skirts on the side in a kind of a bow or knot—the men have no knot and it is smoothly wrapped around them. Older men wear a pink handkerchief on their heads. I think this is a good thing to know.

Whoever sells black umbrellas to the Burmese is making a fortune. I think they are a status symbol—almost everyone carries one. They do protect from the sun and rain. Sun on the face darkens the skin, which they try to avoid.

October 23. *"Point A" Burma* (near Toungoo). *The first American Volunteer Group is still in Burma, and we are not very happy about it. It is too hot. Prices are high to us, since the Burmese think we are rich. When we first came here, one of our guys bought a fresh pineapple for one pie—about one sixth of an American cent. Now they ask a rupee or thirty cents from us.*

A native can live very well on a salary of thirty rupees a month, since food is cheap and the local houses are not too difficult to build.

A family scene in the Shan Hills.

A Burmese temple in Rangoon.

The famous reclining Buddha in Rangoon.

Mr. Kline is an American Baptist missionary who works among the Karens. He says that their legends tell that they came from Tibet or northern China around 600 B.C. He reports that they look like American Indians. Their language is not related to Burmese or Chinese, yet they use "moo" for mother and "pa" for father, which is similar to the Chinese but also like Sanskrit.

October 25. *Pete Atkinson was killed today in a training accident. I was lying on my bed reading when Walt Dolan came by to tell me. This has really shaken up the ground men, for Pete was one of the most popular pilots. He went out of his way to make friends with everyone and was keenly interested in our maintenance problems.*

November 1. *Many stories float over the East that add much to the appreciation of the local scene. The color line is always present, although all races seem to be polite and considerate in the daily rounds.*

An Italian priest in Burma told this story of a family of Anglo-Indians—people of mixed English and native blood. The mother was almost white while the father was very dark. They had three children, two almost black and one very white. The white boy always referred to the woman as "his" mother, but when speaking of the father of the family, he said "their" father.

November 2. *Our accident record is horrible. Besides the three pilots that have been killed in accidents, which took out four planes, we have had many landing crack-ups. The navy pilots think they are landing "big-boats." And we have no spare parts. We steal from the wrecks to keep the other planes flying. The worst problem is tires—when they go, we have no replacements. I am in charge of radio supplies, so I typed a list of the spare parts we need, making five copies. Every time a visiting fireman drops in to see us, I give him a copy. I don't know if it will do any good, but it can't hurt.*

November 4. *Yesterday was another Burmese holiday, so Dolan and I went to see the show in the big pagoda in Toungoo. The Burmese stayed all night but we had to leave early. There are a number of shrines in the pagoda compound, all with a cup for donations. I distributed a few annas, hoping for good luck. We were very welcome. Our guide was Archibald Conar, an Indo-Burman who was born here. We caused more excitement than the dancers. I bought a statue of Bo Ba U, a Burmese saint.*

December 8. *Japan attacked Pearl Harbor and the Philippines today. The AVG is going around in circles. I heard the news about eight in the morning at our headquarters office. I had planned to go into Toungoo and scrounge for tools at the local shops, for we needed screwdrivers, pliers and all sorts of odds and ends. I*

A Burmese home near Toungoo.

Native troops near Toungoo.

One of the many accidents at Toungoo. The pilot overshot the field.

Bore sighting a P-40 at Toungoo. This picture was taken by J.J. Pietsker, AVG photographer, who also played a good game of chess.

Armstrong's funeral at Toungoo. The local Anglican priest assisted our chaplain Paul Frillman.

hesitated a moment, then decided that we were going to need them more than ever. I found a few things we could use, stopped at the railroad station restaurant for a dish of ice cream that was flavored with rose petals and went back to the base.

December 9. *Colonel Chennault offered one squadron to the British to help defend Rangoon. The British refused because they had no place to house the AVG.*

December 10. *The British accepted. The Third Squadron or "Hell's Angels" is being sent to Rangoon. Arvid Olson is the squadron commander. They are taking twenty-one planes and the ground crew. One rumor says that an English officer suggested that we remove the Chinese twelve-pointed blue star from our planes. The AVG reaction to this proposal was not at all favorable.*

December 11. *We are going to abandon Toungoo! Everyone is happy to be going to China. Truck convoys are being organized to carry our supplies and other gear. We are going to use Burmese or Indian drivers for the trucks. We will go up the Burma Road through Lashio.*

We are on a twenty-four hour alert. The planes on the field are kept ready for immediate takeoff at all times. As I lie in my bunk at night, I can hear the engines being warmed up by our mechanics. It gives me a feeling of protection.

Chaplain Frillman officiates at another funeral at Toungoo.

We had our first air raid alarm last night. We went out to the trenches near the barracks, but I was more afraid of the snakes than Japanese bombs. We sent four P-40s up, but it turned out to be a false alarm.

Chennault sent three planes on a reconnaissance mission over Thailand. Newkirk, Merritt and Mangleberg were the pilots. We heard a report that Japanese troops are heading toward Burma from Thailand.

December 12. *I helped set up another transmitter and receiving station at an old building at the end of the field. This is for an emergency in case the main station near the bamboo control tower is bombed. The transmitter is a good one, made by RCA. It has four crystal-controlled channels, and the output is 400 watts.*

December 18. *Our planes left today. The First Squadron with Robert Sandell as commanding officer and the Second Squadron under Jack Newkirk both took off heading north for Kunming, China.*

December 20. *We left the AVG airdrome for Kunming, China, at 10:30 a.m. Our convoy has six International trucks with native drivers and two 1941 Studebakers with four Americans. Willy Sutherland, an auto mechanic, is in charge. Ken Moss and I share one sedan. Ken Breedon is riding with Willy.*

December 22. *7:30 a.m. Burma time. We came to a detour. The British sign called it a "Diversion." We found a truck overturned and it's one of ours. It is the second time since Toungoo that we have found an overturned truck. With the help of some natives from the nearest village and another truck we righted it. We got oil from a local service station to replace what was lost when it turned over. The truck started right away and, aside from a few dents and scratches, seems okay. It was noon before we got started again. We stopped at Kyauske (pronounced Chowsay) for lunch, but as there was no place for foreigners to eat, we opened some cans and ate by the side of the road.*

December 22. *Maymo, Burma. We spent last night in a Chinese-owned hotel in Mandalay. The town was oriental, dirty and drab. Kipling should have forgotten the name. I think the only reason that he used it in his poem was because it rhymed with "flying fishes play." The hotel was a hole. It will be better to sleep in the open air on our cots beside the trucks.*

The drive to Maymyo was perfect. There are hills for the first time since we landed in Burma. It is cooler. The road is good, and the air is clear. The view of the valley behind is superb. Maymyo is a clean town, an English resort where the British escape the heat of the river valley. They even have sidewalks on the main street! There are lots of native pony carts but no rickshaws or tri-shaws, which is a bicycle

Truck accidents were common on the Burma Road. I counted hundreds of such accidents, many in deep gorges. This one happened in the evacuation of Loiwing. A Chinese driver was coasting down a hill at a high rate of speed to save gasoline.

taxi with a side car. We enjoyed a typical English lunch at the Foster Hotel. Ox carts make driving interesting, to say the least.

We met the fellows from the convoy that started the day after we did. They are spending the day and night here—bright boys!

2:30 p.m. We had to stop; the bridge is out. This is beautiful country. Rushing mountain streams wind around the hills. The cool air combined with warm sun reminds me of Colorado. The soil is red here. There are many trees and thick underbrush on either side of the winding road.

We spent the night in a small village about sixty miles south of Lashio. We drank tea in a native hut, the local tea shop. I opened a can of pork and beans and a tin of crackers. We ate with the natives watching. They told us the name of the town was "Bojo." We do not have a road map, and the villages are not marked. We went to bed on our cots beside the trucks.

December 23. *Tea at the native shop, we skipped breakfast. The dew was very heavy last night, and our blankets are wet. My feet got cold. Our clothes aren't warm enough. 9:50 a.m. We stopped to let the other trucks and Willy in the Studebaker catch up with us. We are driving on red roads through rolling, hilly forest. Great* *clumps of poinsettias grow wild at the side of the highway. They are in bloom and add the only holiday atmosphere we have seen. A monkey ran across the road in front of the car. Red dust over green shrubs makes a purplish tinge; we ride over purple hills. There are no palm trees now; the people look more Chinese than Burmese. Their skins are lighter, and they wear trousers instead of skirts. We have not had breakfast yet. I ate a bar of chocolate. The sun has come out and the fog dispersed. It is warmer. It is impossible to drive at night since the fog, dust and an occasional oxcart on the winding road make it too dangerous.*

Yesterday we descended into a gorge and made fifteen tight, steep hairpin curves to get out. I stopped the car half way up and watched the seven trucks below. Several could not make the curves at the first try, but the drivers had to back up to get around. If they had backed up an inch or so too far, they would have rolled hundreds of feet to the river below. It is dangerous but interesting. One cannot be bored on the Burma Road.

December 24. *Lashio. We are actually in New Lashio, a recently built part of a very ancient city. We are staying at a Chinese hotel of better variety. It is very clean. The furniture is made of wicker work and wood. We get tea in the morning instead of hot water. We have a balcony with a view of the valley, the wooded Shan hills and the new town. The air is like Colorado's. It is cold at night, and we do not have enough blankets. I need an overcoat. There are more Chinese than Burmese or British. Lashio is a busy place; the atmosphere and activity are like those of an early Western American boom town. The bazaar is full of goods that probably will be smuggled into China. There are many cars and trucks, all in a hurry, speeding through the winding streets, sounding their horns. There are many Chinese officials, British officers and American civilians here, all involved in pushing trucks and supplies up the Burma Road. Sikh troops from India, Anzaks, Kachin infantrymen, British ratings and Americans of the Chinese Air Force mingle amazingly well in this far off corner of the world. There are P-40s in the air carrying the blue Chinese star flown by pilots from Hamilton and Mitchell fields.*

We had breakfast at the International Cafe that is operated by Chinese. The food is good; I had hot cakes and syrup. For dinner last night we had fried rice, shrimp, fish and chicken fried in hot fat. We had British beer to drink. A Chinese officer paid for our dinners. We could not pay for anything. He said we came to fight for China.

While Lashio is full of new buildings, the hotels are full. We were lucky to get a room. The CNAC (Chinese National Airways Corporation) hostel charges eighteen rupees a day for board and room, or about six American dollars. There is no night life here. The Chinese have their wives with them. There are no women of ill-repute and not much whiskey.

I tried out my new and shaky Chinese on a small boy playing in the hall. I said; "Ni hou bu hou." He replied quickly, "Okay."

Reports filter in from our squadron at Rangoon and the group at Kunming. Six bombers were shot down by the AVG planes at Kunming, and nine bombers and one Japanese fighter were bagged at Rangoon. Rumor says we lost three planes in Rangoon and two pilots, Harry Gilbert and Neil Martin. There were no losses at Kunming.

We are invited out tonight for cocktails at the home of an American oilman who works here. He told us that he called Rangoon this morning on the phone. There was no answer, and usually there are 100 people in his office. There must have been an air raid there this morning. We have not seen any Japanese planes here. We do not have a radio, and the only newspapers are in Chinese. Most of the AVG have their own guns. I do not, but Wyatt lent me a .22 rifle to carry.

December 25. *Christmas. So what? I was up at 8 a.m. to eat a breakfast of four eggs, coffee, toast and jam at a local cafe. Last night we had dinner at Jim Hezzer's, an oil company employee, and played poker for very small stakes with several Americans who work here. We used Chinese silver dollars that our host had collected. Since the "chips" were worth many times our stakes, he counted them carefully before and after our game. Chinese silver dollars are no longer in circulation, since inflation is rampant and the paper money has driven coins out of use. It's a good example of Gresham's Law.*

So far the AVG has had fifty-two major accidents and three pilots killed. Some of the planes have been repaired and others used for spare parts. This is not counting what we may have lost in combat. When the planes took off the other day, December 18 I think, one barely got off the ground, then cracked up at the end of the runway. Another pilot taxied his ship into a car; the propeller cut the car's rear body completely off in four and one-half inch strips. The propeller was, of course, ruined, and we have no spares. Many of the accidents have been due to carelessness on the part of the mechanics and pilots.

Rangoon had another air raid yesterday.

The less one says about the toilet facilities, the better.

December 26. *We were up at seven o'clock and finally left Lashio at 9:30. We now have twelve trucks, one gas truck and four sedans since we have joined another convoy. Ken and I still lead the pack. Bill Seiple is driving the gas truck. We pass many clumps of poinsettias and bamboo, but no more palms. We are climbing up from the valley of the Irrawaddy River and the ancient town of Lashio. The road is winding and tortuous. We pass many pagodas, but the architecture is different with more Chinese influence. There are yellow flowers beside the road that are something like the sunflowers of Kansas. The road is dusty. We passed Shan villages* *where women sat in the dust selling oranges. We stopped and bought some—they were good. Chinese and Burmese coolies are working on the road with meager tools, a wicker basket, and a piece of iron or so. In Chinese the word coolie means literally "bitter work." They smooth the gravel with their hands. We stopped at the village of Ktkai for lunch.*

We arrived at the Burmese border town of Khotkok—it is a Kachen name. It is a collection of small bamboo-roofed shacks run by the Chinese from CAMCO's factory at Loiwing. We were taken in by Mr. White, the British officer in charge of customs at the border. All seven of us slept on our own cots all over his new bunga-low. He furnished us with three quarts of Scotch and a fire in a stone fireplace and told tales of the road. He said he closed the border for three days some months ago. Eight hundred trucks were parked on the Burma side waiting to get through the border. He has a great deal of power. The Chinese border guards had come down and beaten up the Burmese guards. He reports the road is in bad shape ahead. Springs are easily broken, and the top speed is twenty miles an hour.

Mr. White is at first glance white, but he has dark eyes with sort of a liquid look of the natives of India. His hair is dark and slightly curly. He is six feet tall, weighs one hundred eighty pounds and is very jovial. He has a definite "English" accent and is in favor of the "supremacy of the white race." The next morning he appeared wearing a pink shirt—an Englishman would not do that in Burma.

He is very shocked at the behavior of the AVG personnel, for reports have filtered to the border of our actions. We drink native rice wine and associate with native women. Mr. White referred to us as white coolies. Mr. White's assistant is an Anglo-Burman, who wears a native skirt when he is out of uniform. There is a close bond between them—they may be brothers.

Our Chinese interpreter, M.B. Tong, speaks English with an American accent. He is the supply officer for CAMCO at Loiwing. He likes whiskey and cigarettes. He worries about us and our actions. He has never been to the United States but wants to send his fourteen-year-old son there to college. He is going to work in AVG supply in Kunming. His wife and one son are with us, riding in Sutherland's sedan.

The odometer on my Studebaker sedan reads 02146. When we left Toungoo, it read 01154, which means we have traveled 992 kilometers to reach the border.

We changed our Burmese rupees to Chinese dollars. The black market of Khotkok paid $15.50 Chinese for one rupee. I have less than a thousand Chinese dollars due to many expenses and the loss of a few rupees at poker. The bank rate is seven to one for rupees. There is no black market here for American dollars. Since we get three rupees, four annas for a dollar, that makes a Chinese dollar worth two cents. There are few coins in circulation—I have not seen any yet.

Our interpreter, M.B. Tong or, in the Chinese fashion Tong Ming Bau, is most helpful in the currency transactions. His English is very good. We were given Chi-

nese drivers for our trucks in Lashio; the Burmese were paid off. We ate lunch at a small village in a cafe designed to cater to the passing Chinese truck drivers. It is built of bamboo with dirt floors. M.B. Tong ordered boiling water and scalded the bowls and chopsticks before he would let us eat from them. He told us to always eat hot food that had just been cooked.

The lunch consisted of eggs that had been pickled in lime—the yolks were dark green and the whites transparent—abalone, cuttle fish or octopus, curried chicken, and a kind of fried black flour that looked horrible but tasted good. We also had vegetables, rice and soup. We all ate with chopsticks, as there were no knives or forks.

December 27. *9:00 a.m. There is a large river to the left of us. We filled up with gas on the China side and left at 8:45. At ten o'clock we reached the town of Chufan. We stopped to leave various papers with the Chinese authorities regarding our convoy.*

There are quite a few foreigners on the road. This morning at breakfast besides the seven of the AVG, there were about ten British Red Cross men and five or six American missionaries, including two women. Seeing us eating a kind of dumpling filled with curried chicken and bean sprouts, one of the women ordered it also.

Burma Road is good so far. It is surfaced. There was a heavy fog over the mountain by the border, but now the valley of the river is clear. There many of the local Shan women dressed in black leggings, black kilts, blouses and high head-dresses.

Mr. White had a radio, and we learned that Hong Kong had fallen to the Japanese, the British have captured Benghazi, Churchill is in Washington and the Germans are still retreating in Russia. We also heard that the AVG had been doing well in Rangoon with nineteen Japanese planes shot down. Rangoon was bombed three times, and the casualties were heavy. Kunming was also bombed and lost a lot of people on December 18; our planes came in a few hours after the raid.

Height of futility: trying to dodge ruts on the Burma Road and also writing in this diary. Ken Moss is driving. We take turns at it. Ken is a weather man.

Mengshih, 1 p.m. We stopped for lunch. Major Lwoh, the commander of the garrison, paid for it. We had Chinese food and no knives or forks. We have to learn to eat with chopsticks or starve here. Concessions to us were soup served first and cocoa. The soup contained chicken lungs and other parts of the chicken and some items that were unrecognizable. It was good, however.

3 p.m. We stopped, for there was a truck in the ditch. Fortunately it was not one of ours. One of our Studebaker sedans also has gear trouble and cannot move. Willy is trying to fix it, and meanwhile there are trucks stacked up for miles on the highway on either side of the scene.

The valley of the Mangshih is famous for its malaria. Thousands died of it here when the road was built. Mosquitoes breed in the bamboo. Since this is December, we are not bothered by them.

3:10 p.m. We moved the stalled sedan to the side of the road and left Willy Sutherland—our auto mechanic—with it. Breedon, who is driving another sedan, and Seiple on the gas truck stayed too. The rest of us decided to go ahead and wait at the next town, which is only a few miles away.

4:00 p.m. We arrived at Leonglin and will stay here tonight. We went to the motor pool and waited for the other two cars and the gas truck. At 4:15 they pulled in. We went to the New Light Hotel and got a room containing six beds for only ten dollars Chinese each. Breedon slept on his cot, so he did not have to pay. Ken and I opened a can of beans, peas and pineapple and ate them with cheese and crackers. I got out the pot, and the Chinese house boy made the coffee for us. I opened a can of real cream from Australia. The hotel is new with white walls. It is made of mud bricks and has dirt floors and is built around a courtyard. We all went to bed at seven o'clock.

December 28. *Sunday. We were up at 5:30 a.m. It is still Burma time. We drank a cup of coffee and went out to the trucks to check on the drivers. At 6:45 we were waiting for gas for two or three of them. A group of Chinese soldiers were washing their faces with a wet cloth, passing it from one to the other. Petrol tins are piled high in the compound. Fifty or more trucks are parked in the lot. It is foggy and we are cold and damp.*

Yesterday we saw five or six wrecks. Some of the trucks were hundreds of feet below, lodged among the boulders. The road is carved out of solid rock on the mountain. In some places it is very narrow and always rough. It is several thousand feet to the valley below. Sometimes it is paved with asphalt or oil; mostly it is rough cobblestones. I wonder how our radio equipment will make the trip to Kunming.

M.B. Tong says we should get to Kunming in five days or the first of January, 1942. We want to get to Paoshan tonight, about 200 kilometers. We only traveled 120 kilometers yesterday. It is 846 kilometers to Kunming from here.

10.45 a.m. The Fifth Route Chinese Army is passing us going south to help defend Rangoon. It has artillery.

11:30 a.m. We arrived at the Waytong Bridge over the Lukiang River. The Japanese have tried time and again to bomb the bridge. Thousands of tons of explosives have been dropped near it, but it still stands. It is very narrow; only one truck at a time can cross it one way. It is a suspension bridge fifty-two meters long. Bamboo has been wrapped around the steel cables to protect it from bomb hits. In case the bridge is destroyed, the Chinese have built another road down to the river where trucks can be ferried across the Lukiang River. We had to stop so that the Army could pass. The Japanese have given up trying to bomb the bridge. The deep can-

The Burma Road near the Salween River.

The Burma Road climbing up from the Salween River gorge.

The suspension bridge over the Salween River.

yon and surrounding high hills protect it. When they were bombing it, the trucks waited at nearby towns during the raids. The Chinese have an air raid warning net all over these mountains, using both telephone and radio. The warning gives them enough time to avoid the bridge during a raid.

The river is very green, a reflection of the mountains and pine trees. The bridge used to be six feet higher than the road. Now it is about six feet below the road. The Chinese keep tightening the cables as they stretch. The floats for the emergency ferry are made of fifty gallon gas drums.

A tablet near the bridge says "17 feet wide, 100 feet high, 368 feet long." It was built January 31, 1935. The stone was erected by the Leong Ling people. Eighteen two-inch cables hold the bridge, nine on each side. The tablet is in Chinese, so M.B. Tong translated it for me. The British engineer in charge was named but in Chinese characters. It sounds something like "Polan Sue Carson." The Chinese had built another bridge here about 100 years ago.

12:05 p.m. We are 1,000 feet above the river. At a narrow curve two trucks meet. The red road is cut out of solid rock. We stop and watch to see if the trucks can pass. There is no railing and only a sheer cliff at our left. The trucks creep slowly past while avoiding disaster. The road is carved out of the hillside, full of narrow, twisting curves. The view of the small valley far below with the road winding around

Another picture of the Salween River bridge.

The Salween River bridge from downriver.

the mountains is a memorable sight. The sun is bright and warm, the air clear and cool. The road itself, while narrow and dangerous at many spots, is generally wide enough for two trucks to pass. It is cut through territory where only a narrow burro trail went before. It is a magnificent engineering feat. The road was built and is maintained by whole families who live near it.

4 p.m. We arrived at Paoshan and stopped at the air field outside the walled city. Miller, an AVG radioman, is stationed all alone here in charge of our station. I decided to spend the night with him. Miller and I were in the 20th Pursuit Group at Hamilton Field. I discovered that he did not drink or smoke. He had been converted by some local missionaries and did not approve at all of the actions of some of our group. He had dismissed his cook and fixed dinner for me cooking over a charcoal pot. He had not been paid for two months.

He works closely with the Chinese air raid warning net, relaying any reports of enemy action to our headquarters in Kunming. He has a large map of Yunnan Province with a super imposed grid. The top of the map is divided into sections labeled "A," "B," "C," and so on. At the left side of the map the sections are numbered. He reports the enemy activity by the grid designation: for example, "Heavy engine noise in sector D-15." There is either a Chinese telephone or radio station in each section of the grid.

This Paoshan valley is very beautiful and fertile. After the hot sticky weather of lowland Burma, the climate is excellent. It reminds me somewhat of the American west. It could be a vacation attraction if it were modernized. I was told that there is coal in the nearby mountains. Most of the pine trees near the town have been cut down for fuel. Marco Polo came through Paoshan on his way to Burma.

December 29. *10:30 a.m. The first air raid alarm sounded, one long and two short blasts. We were at the station trying to contact Colonel Chennault at Kunming. Some of our trucks were to return to Lashio. Sutherland decided to send them back without authorization. We went to the spot where our trucks were parked, but our drivers had all gone out on the north road due to the alarm. Our three cars are parked by the city wall. The six of us built a fire and made coffee. We ate our lunch out of cans. At noon the second alarm sounded. We finished our coffee hastily and went out on the north road. We found M.B. Tong and the trucks and waited there for the all clear.*

We decided to stay all night. I went out to see Miller, who gave me coffee and peanuts.

December 30. *We left Paoshan at eight o'clock. We climbed mountain roads and passed women in bound feet breaking rocks with a small iron hammer. They put gravel in small piles. It will be used for repair of the road. It takes so many hours—days or months of tedious work by so many people to maintain the Burma Road.*

Bob Locke on a ferry over the Salween River after evacuating Loiwing.

Walt Dolan and his dog Oscar crossing the Salween from Loiwing.

Ancient crones pass carrying great bundles of wood on their backs, barely able to walk with their tiny feet. They use a stick to support part of the weight. I had always thought that only the rich Chinese women had bound feet, but even the poorest of them who must work have the tiny "lily" feet. Women with bound feet are all over forty years old, for the practice was stopped when the last empress was deposed.

Long burro trains are at the side of the road, carrying heavy packs from Bahmo in Burma. Coolies carry large bundles slung from a pole over their shoulders.

We stopped at a small town for lunch at a primitive restaurant. We had rice, Chinese chicken, vegetables, bean curd and soup. It cost $34 Chinese for six of us or about 70¢ in our money. I bought some oranges for $1.50 Chinese money each. We heard that Kunming is to be the ABCD (American, British, Chinese and Dutch) headquarters. I hope this is true for it will mean that we will stay there.

Miller told me that the local authorities caught several Chinese stealing small odds and ends from the trucks passing through. The culprits were lined up against a wall and shot. He said that a Chinese officer and an enlisted man showed an American a house of ill repute. The private was shot and the captain docked two months pay. Life is cheap here.

We are driving past Chinese villages built of mud bricks, thatched roofs, terraced rice fields flooded with water prior to planting and plots of beans and chards.

December 31. We slept last night in the guest house of Lungling. It was kind of a hole. The beds were of wood, including the springs. I spread my bedroll over the bed as usual to avoid contact with the mattress, such as it was. I ate two eggs, fried to order, with chopsticks. Eating eggs with two sticks of bamboo is almost hopeless unless one is starving and gets help from his fingers. I opened a can of beans and asparagus and had the boy heat them for us. For heating the charge was two Chinese dollars; for the eggs, three dollars.

I spent yesterday afternoon reading The Damned Don't Cry by Harry Hervey. For light in the evening we had an ancient oil lamp with a wick sticking out of one end. The Greeks three thousand years ago had a better one. The other fellows played poker with Chinese dollars.

We were up at 6:30 to start around eight o'clock. We found more dust-filled roads winding around the Yunnan hills. There is snow on the mountains in the distance. The hill people of the province are working on the road, looking like gnomes, short, stunted and clad in blue rags. Many of them have large goiters on their necks, caused by the lack of iodine in their diet. All are ill fed and poverty stricken in a way that makes our poor look like millionaires.

10:30 a.m. We stopped for coffee at Taibingfu. I took the pot to a native cafe with the makings and with hot water from a big kettle and brewed a good batch. As we have had no water for days, we must drink coffee or tea. Sometimes we open a can of milk and make cocoa. We have not had any water or ice since Toungoo. As I write this, some of the Yunnanese stand by the car watching us. They don't seem to understand our attempts to say hello. Some of the buildings are log cabins with tile roofs. Others are thatched with straw. There is more goiter present. The mountains are covered with pines, and clear mountain streams rush over rocky beds.

11:00 a.m. We stopped for a few minutes to enjoy the view. The road looks like a white ribbon, winding its way thousands of feet into the valley below. The air is clear, the sky bright and blue with white bands of clouds balanced on the high snow-covered peaks. The pine forest is very fragrant. This reminds me so much of the Rocky Mountains of western Colorado. But something else is added, terraced rice fields on the mountain slopes and native clay igloos, Mongolian faces above clothing of blue rags, and a temple on a nearby hill. And then, too, there's plenty of Yunnan dust in clouds behind American trucks on the Burma Road. Chinese soldiers are riding south to battle at Rangoon, reminding us we are not tourists making a luxury cruise but part of the vast scheme of World War II.

1:30 p.m. We arrived at Saikwan to stay at the local "guest house." After a meal of hot Ovaltine, cold beans and peas, canned ham and crackers and sardines, we left the trucks and went to the city of Tali on a sightseeing tour. It used to be called Talifu, the fu meaning a local capital under the Empire. It is a very famous city in China and was visited by Marco Polo. It is a source of marble. There is a large native market filled with eager buyers and sellers. We met some Assembly of God missionaries; one was American and one British. They have been here eleven years, and their station is thirteen days by horseback up in the mountains—about 250 miles.

We met about fifteen Tibetans in the street. They are pilgrims from the land of mystery that is forbidden to foreigners. There is a mountain near here that is sacred to them, and they visit it on pilgrimages. I wonder what drives them to make this long trip on foot to Tali. Perhaps the local market is one attraction, for they can buy things here that are not available in Tibet. They were dressed in shaggy wools, their feet encased in fur-lined boots, carrying staffs tipped with long knives. They had packs on their backs and were accompanied by their women. The men were sturdy, though not tall. They had wide shoulders and long black hair that fell over their eyes. This is really romance, with a capital R. I feel a longing to go back to Tibet with these travelers and see the forbidden city of Lhasa.

There is a great lake just east of Tali called Ur Hi. It is a beautiful blue and many miles long.

As I write this, it's after five o'clock and I am back at our hotel in Saikwan. This place is also strange and romantic. I am on a balcony overlooking a roughly paved courtyard. Water and other unwanted debris are flung over the rail; let those below beware. Four unhappy looking palm trees grow in four pots. A parrot, who must be freezing, sits discontentedly upon his perch. The roofs are tile, a dirty black color, with the ends turned up in Chinese fashion. A Chinese boy wearing a dark blue robe that almost touches the floor laughs with another in western dress. A girl with bright oblique eyes smiles from the other balcony. The sun is low in the sky and the air is cold, warning of frost tonight.

January 1, 1942. We were up at 6:30 to start about 7:30. We left the lake, which is forty-seven miles long, and entered a small pass which leads into a broader valley.

10:30 a.m. We arrived at the AVG hostel at Yunnanyi. We found Ernie Bonham, our radio operator here, at the mess hall, where we had breakfast. The buildings are new and clean. The tables have white cloths, shining silver and good American style ham and eggs and coffee. We can buy Camel cigarettes at the hostel. The bathrooms have showers and hot water.

The Chinese are building a new hostel here for one thousand Americans. They are building other such hostels all over free China.

Rumor says that the United States will send 1,000 planes to China plus personnel and equipment in exchange for the Chinese troops sent to Rangoon and Malaya.

The ancient temple where we spent the night on the way up the Burma Road at Tsu-Yung, January 1, 1942.

*The AVG has had thirty-two victories to date, perhaps more that were not cred-
ited. The United States and China are hearing a lot about the AVG now.*

*Lacy Mangleburg was killed on December 24 at Lotienshang Po. He and Shil-
ling and Merritt were flying three CW-21s up to Kunming and ran into some terrible weather. We lost all three planes. Shilling and Merritt brought their ships in
for crash landings. That makes six pilots we have lost so far but only two in combat.*

*We arrived at Tsuyung about 4:30 p.m. We were met by the AVG interpreter,
who took us to Captain Chen, the commanding officer of the local air field. Captain
Lieu from Yunnanyi was also there to greet us. They took us to an old temple built in
the Ming Dynasty, where we spent the night. The Ta Chung temple had not been
used for years until it was made into a barracks for about 100 Chinese air cadets
last year. The ancient moat just inside the outer wall was spanned by several bridges
of stone. The court yards are roughly paved with stone and have several pine trees
growing in the corners. Lions and other figures of animals carved from marble
decorate the walls. The roofs are tile. There are ancient inlay works on the ceilings
in many bright colors. We slept well in this temple dedicated to Kung Fu Tze. Westerners call him Confucius.*

*Captains Chen and Lieu treated us royally. They took us to dinner at a local
restaurant where we had pork chops, fried eggs, good coffee and rice wine. We call
the wine "white lightning" and another type "green death." We were then invited
to Captain Chen's house to play poker. Captain Chen does not speak English. Captain Lieu has lived most of his life in New York and Florida; he would like to go
back.*

January 2. *I was up at seven and had a breakfast of scrambled eggs and pork, hot
meat-filled dumplings and coffee. We picked up Dr. May, a Chinese who was educated at Johns Hopkins, and four air cadets who wanted a ride to Kunming. We left
Tsuyung at 8:30 a.m. It is 185 kilometers to Kunming, and we should get there this
afternoon. We have two mountain ranges to cross.*

*From the tales I've heard of the Burma Road I had expected bombs, bandits,
headhunters and impassable barriers. But so far the road has been a pleasant surprise. Of course there were places with a truck on one side of us and death on the
other with sheer drops of thousands of feet and roads so rough that five miles per
hour would have been difficult. The red dust has covered everything, getting in our
food, throats and clothes, yet the trip was much easier than I had expected.*

1:00 p.m. We stopped for lunch at Lufung.

*4:30. We arrived at Kunming and found ourselves assigned to a large barracks
with hot showers and a real bar on the second floor. The food is good; it is a wonderful place to stay. The building used to be a college. We are assigned two to a
room.*

The men from the "Fighting Third Squadron" just came in from two weeks' battle in Rangoon. They report that at least fifty-two Japanese bombers were knocked down. There were two major bomb raids while they were there. One of the ground crew was still shaken.

"It was horrible, Smitty, it was horrible," he said. "Sixty-five tons of bombs were dropped on Rangoon. It was worse than anything the British saw at London. I never want to see another like it. The Japanese hit everything, operations, the heart of the field. They hit the fake petrol dump and the real one, the power station, our barracks, the mess hall, everything. They got a couple of our planes on the ground.

Our pilots really fought. We were 'Burma' that day. We shot down fifty-two Jap planes and many went into the bay. I was near the docks; I saw them go in.

Get on your face in a ditch, that's all you can do—and pray. You can't fight back; you want to run, anyplace, anywhere, just run. It wouldn't be so bad if you could do something; you're so helpless, Smitty.

There was a Hindu and a Mohammedan in our trench. The Hindu was praying to Vishnu, the Mohammedan to Allah; we were praying too, all of us.

Every man standing up on the field was killed. You've got to get down on your face in a ditch. Only a direct hit will get you then.

When it was all over, I hated to go back. I didn't want to know who got theirs. I didn't want to see the field.

You remember, Smitty, that good looking red-headed private at Toungoo? He was transferred to Mingladon. He got it. Direct hit. He was in the operations office. I saw parts of him hanging from a barbed wire fence. Oh, it was horrible, Smitty, horrible. I never want to see it again.

We didn't have anything to eat for days except bread. The mess hall was bombed. The servants were gone. Yes, Rangoon is walking back to India. There are 150,000 Indians, barefooted and on bicycles, in rickshaws, some of them driving a cow, going up the road to Mandalay, then across to Assam. The coolies at the docks are gone. We can't unload the ships. I saw English regiments moving cargo.

That is a sight, Rangoon walking back to India.

It was the greatest aerial victory in history for one fighter squadron. But it was hell, sixty-five tons of bombs, big stuff.

You ought to see the craters; you could hide a car in one of them.

I was in a drain pipe under a bridge. One bomb hit on one side, then one on the other. Big red ants were crawling all over me.

Did they bite me? I don't know. I shook them off afterwards.

Where were the British on the first raid? I don't know.

The New Zealand pilots were wonderful, and some of the British sergeant pilots did all right on the second raid.

Bob Locke's pet leopard on the nose of a P-40. The cat was later killed in an accident on the Burma Road.

R. M. Smith with Bob Locke's pet.

We lost two pilots, Neil Martin and Henry Gilbert. I think the British antiair-craft shot Gilbert down. It was the only thing they did all day. It had to be one of ours.

P.J. Green bailed out. The Japs tried to get him as he came down in his chute. We were praying for him, every last one of us. He got down okay. Martin never fired a shot. He got caught in the cross-fire of the Japs. It was bad. He didn't have a chance."

January 3. *While I was on the Burma Road, the AVG had its first victory south of Kunming. Ten Japanese two-engined bombers took off from Hanoi a little after nine o'clock in the morning. The Chinese air raid warning net picked them up early, but there was a heavy overcast, and many of the reports were "heavy engine noise." Planes from both the First and Second Squadrons took part in the action. Fritz Wolf got two bombers. Bob Neale, Hoffman and Sandell each shot one down. The Chinese net reported that only four of the Japanese planes crossed the border on their way home and that only one landed in Hanoi. That's almost a perfect score. Ed Rector ran out of gas and had to land in a rice paddy. It took him a week to get back to Kunming.*

A water wheel in Yunnan near the Burma Road.

A Chinese junk on the lake at Kunming. The lake is about fifty miles long and ten miles wide.

January 4. *Marion F. Baugh was killed yesterday on the way to Yunnanyi in an accident in a Ryan ST. Julian Terry was with him and pinned in the wreckage by the engine. He was hurt badly. Baugh did not sign up for the AVG, but was hired as an instructor for a flight school.*

January 6. *Kunming. 6:20 p.m. I was in bed all morning nursing the hole where a tooth used to be. It was abscessed and had to come out. I took an ounce of castor oil yesterday and eight pills of sulfathiazole. I went to the warehouse this afternoon to try to organize our supplies.*

On January 4 three of our planes raided Bangkok in Thailand. Three Japanese fighters on an air patrol and four planes on the field were destroyed. Newkirk, Hill and Howard were the pilots.

The next day over forty Japanese fighters and over twenty bombers came over Rangoon in retaliation. We lost three ships, but no pilots. Five Japanese planes were shot down. The AVG were ready for war. We have been in intensive training since August. The British at Rangoon were not. They were poorly organized. There was no food for the AVG or British pilots. For three days their rations were bread and beer. They had butter on the bread for one breakfast.

The British air raid net was a mess. The head man of a village would tell the local commissioner, who would then telephone air raid headquarters. Then head-

A street in Kunming.

Happy Chinese boat people on the lake at Kunming.

quarters would check with the AVG and the RAF to see if our planes were in the air. If there were no friendlies in the air, he would call back through channels to the headman to see if he still saw them.

January 10. *Ken Merritt was killed in a horrible accident in Rangoon yesterday. Three of our pilots were doing some night flying, since the Japanese have been sending out their bombers at night, trying to get our planes on the ground. Gil Bright, Jim Howard and Pete Wright were in the air but missed the Japanese. When Pete landed, his hydraulic lines blew out and he lost control of the P-40. Merritt was sleeping in a sedan near the runway. He was killed instantly when Wright's plane ran into the car. Wright was not hurt. We lost another pilot the other day in Rangoon. Charlie Mott did not return from a strafing mission in Thailand.*

January 25. *The Japanese have started to bomb Rangoon again. They sent over sixty planes on the twenty-third. Our pilots got twenty-one of them. Bert Christman was killed in the battle. Bert was a comic strip artist that used to work for Milton Caniff on "Terry and the Pirates." Some of our P-40s were badly damaged.*

January 28. *The air battle over Rangoon is still raging. We are knocking down a lot of Japanese planes, but it is costly. Louis Hoffman was killed two days ago. He was a former navy pilot.*

A back street at Kunming.

January 29. *We heard a report from Rangoon that Charlie Mott is a prisoner of war in Thailand.*

February 4. *Tom Cole was killed recently in a raid on the Japanese field at Meshod near Moulmein in Thailand. He was shot down by ground fire while strafing the field.*

February 9. *Robert Sandell was killed on the seventh in an accident in Rangoon. He was the squadron commander of the First Squadron— the Adam and Eves. Bob Neale has been appointed its new commanding officer, replacing Sandell.*

February 18. *I like Yunnan. It is beautiful country. The valley of Kunming is an entrancing sight from the hills. One sees neat small plots of ground, green with winter wheat and vegetables. There are clumps of pines, villages of adobe and tile. The*

A Chinese woman with a large goiter. Goiters were common in Yunnan, due to the lack of iodine in the soil.

lake is fifty miles long and the water is a deep blue. The cliff of the mountain of Si San rises about 2,000 feet above the valley floor. The winter climate is perfect, better in some ways than that of California or Florida. There is an occasional frost. The noonday sun is always warm and the air clear and pure. There is a scent of pine in the air.

February 19. *Singapore surrendered to the Japanese on the fifteenth.*

February 22. *Scraps of conversation from AVG ground men: "Hedman made a world's record that Christmas Day. He went up and shot down one Jap bomber and had the whole damned canopy shot off his ship. When he landed his gas tanks were full of holes—leaking fast."*

"He went up again in another ship?"

"Yes. He shot down five Jap bombers in one flight. It's a world's record. He lost another canopy, the gas tanks were full of holes again and he was out of ammunition. He's one of the best. The P-40 isn't so bad after all."

"It's better than anything the Japs have. And the Limeys haven't made any records like the AVG."

"They have a lot of P-40s."

"They're all in storage. The Limeys can't fly them."

"I hear Newkirk has twenty-five planes to his credit."

"Twenty-five confirmed. He's got more than that."[1]

"We've shot down more—the AVG alone—than all the American Air Force in the Philippines."

[1] *Newkirk's actual confirmed record was 10.5 planes.*

February 21. *Kunyang, Yunnan, China. I am here for a week to relieve the AVG stationmaster, R. L. Richardson. Rich has a nice setup here. An ancient temple is fixed up for the transmitter; he has a two-room apartment. His Chinese staff consists of one interpreter, one operator, a cook, an orderly and several telephone men to watch the telephone net. The guard is from twenty to thirty Chinese soldiers. He has a dog. The cook turns out good food. The interpreter is intelligent and the orderly amiable if a bit obtuse. The dog sleeps. The furnishings include a bed, comfortable wicker chairs, tables and straw mats for the floors, Chinese prints on the walls make it a homelike atmosphere.*

Rich went to Kunming for a kind of vacation. He has not had a day off since November.

An AVG truck at the motor pool in Kunming.

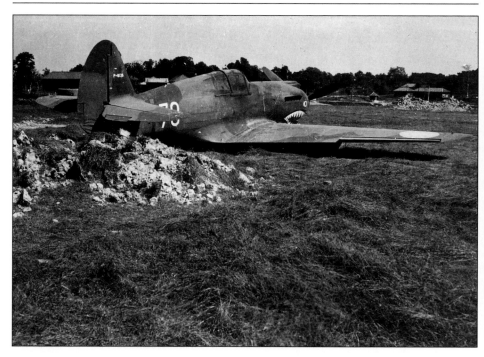

A crash landing after an air battle at Mingladon air field in Rangoon. The picture was taken in February, 1942.

Pete Atkinson's plane after it crashed near Toungoo.

Crash landing at Rangoon. This was Dick Rossi's plane and was abandoned when Rangoon was evacuated.

February 22. *Up at 6:10 to rush over to start the engine and warm up the transmitter. I should have been on the air at 6 a.m. I reported in to Boogie (Ed Baughman) at the net control station in Kunming. Then I went to a breakfast consisting of one very large omelet mixed with vegetables and corned beef, two enormous hot cakes, strawberry jam and coffee. The jam was excellent; it was made locally by some German missionaries. I told the cook to cut down on the breakfast hereafter. He thought that all Americans ate like Richardson.*

Last night, after drinking a small amount of native fruit wine, I went to bed at 9:30. About midnight a call came in reporting engine noise over one of the telephone reporting stations. The operator on duty aroused the interpreter, and they both tried to awaken me. They pounded on the door for fifteen minutes and started the power plant, thus turning on the lights in my room. But I slept on very soundly. After half an hour they gave up and went to bed. Since the station headquarters at Kunming was closed, it wouldn't have done any good to have been awake. My subconscious must have known that.

The Chinese net has a separate line to the Chinese net control station in Kunming, and they could have alerted our people there if it were necessary. Our AVG radio net is interconnected with the Chinese net; our stations are located at their sub-net control stations so that we may get information of Japanese activity as quickly as possible, relaying it to Kunming or to our planes, if necessary. Since our stations and aircraft are all on the same frequency, 6048 kilocycles, all information is shared by headquarters, radio stations and our planes immediately.

This old temple is a romantic spot. It has ancient idols, crumbling tile and adobe brick walls that seem to ignore the wind and rain. The lacquered carvings are colored with brilliant reds, blues and gold. Around the outer wall eucalyptus trees rustle and sway in the wind. Age-old ceremonies are still held here, although the priests left long ago. The new world intrudes into this peaceful spot. Boogie's voice, with his American accent and navy frankness, fills the rough stone paved courtyard, for the loudspeaker of the communications receiver sits on the upstairs balcony so that I can hear transmissions all over the temple.

The roads show the changing way of life in old Yunnan. The roads built under the dynasties centuries ago are narrow, twisting and roughly paved with stone. Those highways were meant for pedestrians, sedan chairs or an occasional pony or two. But the new roads are wide, graveled, straight and smooth. They are not as smooth as an American highway, but cars and trucks make respectable time on them, and they serve their purpose.

It isn't fair to compare the roads of China and those of our land. We should compare the past with today. Then one can see the impact of American civilization. I say American and not Western or European purposely. In China it is the influence of America that is changing the ancient ways. On the Burma Road one sees Ameri-

Another view of Dick Rossi's plane at Rangoon.

A mechanic salvaging parts from plane number three (P-8103). This was standard operating procedure for the AVG.

can trucks, American cars and even the American navy! European cars are about as common as in the United States. I saw only one non-American truck on the trip up the Burma Road. This was in a vacant lot in Lashio, Burma. The truck was British made, several years old and no longer operating.

There's a wedding feast going on out in the temple courtyard. The temple is public property, and the local people of the village entertain their friends here. The feast will last three days. Even if it is a feast the guests eat great quantities of rice. One would think that they would want to eat some thing else for a change at a banquet.

The Chinese take their religion lightly. They make very matter-of-fact uses of their temples; they can be used for barracks for troops, radio stations, headquarters for an army or a vacation villa. This is understandable since the temples are the only public buildings in the villages.

In the courtyard a Chinese is playing a one-stringed violin; a group of the local men are gossiping in one corner; the village deaf-mute is making strange sounds at two dogs otherwise engaged; a small girl of about eight years plays with her friend while carrying a large baby on her back. I sit on the balcony taking it all in.

A "stationmaster" at an AVG radio station has an interesting life until something goes wrong. Then he earns his pay quickly. Generally everything moves

Pilots' alert tent at Mingladon airdrome.

British and AVG pilots waiting at Rangoon for the next Japanese attack.

The barracks at Rangoon used by the AVG.

smoothly, so much so that right now most of the radiomen are on edge. Not to have a day off for three or four months gets monotonous. From some of the all too frank conversations on our frequency, I can tell where I'll go next. Bonham says he doesn't mind talking to himself; when he starts answering, it's time for a holiday. So I'll probably go to Yunnanyi next to give Bonham a chance to go to Kunming and its two restaurants. One is a hole; the other not too bad but with sky high prices. There are two local cinemas, the Nan Ping and the Kun Ming, that show very old American pictures with Chinese subtitles.

The Kuan Ying Tze temple was built in 1905 in the Ching Dynasty, the last dynasty before the revolution.

February 24. *A conversation on our frequency:*
"Hey, Boogie, can't you work on that day off for me?"
"Mr. D's doing that. He's the man."
"I used to like this place. The soldiers had a herd of goats but now they have killed them and made themselves coats."
"I see what you mean."

Armorer Jack Linton waiting for the planes to return.

Robert H. Neale's plane after a battle over Rangoon. Note the many bullet holes. Neale was the top ace in the AVG with fifteen and one-half Japanese planes confirmed.

There is all kinds of American humor on our frequency. Shreffler at Chanyi has a phonograph and puts out jazz once in awhile. Sasser at Mungtze has a fondness for telling the details of his sex life.

February 27. *Richardson returned today from Kunming happy to have "seen the sights" of Kunming. I drove the fifty miles back to Kunming in a Studebaker sedan.*

February 28. *The AVG evacuated Rangoon today. Ed Leibolt is missing.*

February 29. *Last night their Excellencies, Generalissimo and Madame Chiang Kai-shek, gave a dinner in our honor in Kunming.*

I was lucky to be here so I could attend. Both the Generalissimo and Madame spoke—Madame rather stirringly. She called us her "boys," thanked us for the money we had given to her charities, lectured us in a motherly sort of way about our behavior, bragged about us and told us she was very proud of us and proud to be our honorary commander-in-chief.

The Generalissimo called us his "officers and staff members." He told us that we would be accorded all the privileges of Chinese officers and that we were fighting bravely and well. He spoke of our record as a historic accomplishment that had never been equaled by any other group in the history of the world.

AVG pilots at Kunming. They are Dean, Brown, unidentified, Rosbert, Bond, Lebold and Hoffman.

Hostel number one at Kunming. It was a college building before being turned into quarters for the AVG. I shared a room with Ken Moss on the first floor. It had hot showers—a luxury in China.

Ground personnel of the Third Squadron.

Pilots of the Second Squadron.

Colonel Chennault told us that the honor conferred upon our group by this dinner was unprecedented and that no matter what medals or decorations that we received individually or as a group, this was the greatest honor of them all. No great leaders of a powerful nation had ever invited the entire personnel of one organization to a similar affair.

Madame and the Generalissimo were received with a hearty welcome. We are all proud to fight for China.

March 3. *Chanyi, Yunnan. I was sent here for a week or so to relieve Shreffler at the AVG station. Chanyi is about the best of the outlying stations. It has a good landing field and a complete hostel designed for 200 Americans. I am the only one here. It has a full staff of servants, a good stock of wine, excellent food and a nice room. There is even a barber to cut my hair. The transmitter and radio equipment are in top shape.*

March 6. *It looks like I am to stay here for more than a week, perhaps permanently. Shreffler is to help build a direction finder in Kunming and then perhaps install a new radio station in Chungking. If so, I will have to have my clothes—I brought precious little with me.*

A funeral at Kunming. Twenty-two pilots and one ground man were killed in the year that the AVG was in existence.

Gil Bright and three other pilots dropped in for tea in their P-40s the other day. Five of our planes headed this way yesterday but got lost. Three of them made a forced landing at Weyshan near Mungtze. Two others landed in the boondocks. One will have to travel three days by horseback to get to Weyshan.

The military situation looks bad in Java. If we can win there the war could be over in six months. If we lose, who knows how long it will take? I listen to the news in English from Chungking every afternoon at three o'clock. It is followed by news in Chinese—the radio operators cluster around to listen.

March 8. I have nothing to read. However, I have the promise of a Chinese doctor for some books. The doctor spent eight years in the United States and is a graduate of Johns Hopkins. He has some old Reader's Digests. A local colonel of the Chinese Army, whose wife is one-half English, has a store of books. So I have invited him to dinner next Sunday. In fact, I have invited ten people, among them an English Red Cross man.

The Englishman, Sidney Bailey, is much worse off than I am. He has no car, eats Chinese food (it's good but different from ours) and lives in rat-infested quarters. My barracks are new, clean and built of stone and cement. There are glass

Duke Hedman and his P-40.

A dummy P-40 at an outlying field in Yunnan. The Chinese built hundreds of these fake planes of straw and bamboo and scattered them all over China. The Japanese claims of AVG planes destroyed on the ground were generally based on dummies destroyed.

Christman, McClure and Misenheimer working on a P-40.

Osborne, Donovan and Dolan in front of a decoy P-40 at Paoshan.

AVG pilots Jernstedt, Haywood, Older and R. T. Smith. The first three were former United States Marine pilots. The P-40 is R. T. Smith's, showing five "kills."

windows in the hostel; his are made of paper. The paper has to be replaced after a rain.

I just finished dinner. It consisted of a thick vegetable soup, a meat loaf containing chicken, a type of local peas that are green in color and look like lima beans, creamed celery, chip potatoes and excellent hot custard with real maple syrup. To top that off, the boy brought me a banana—I have no idea where it came from—and coffee.

The cook here is one of the best in China and has cooked for Westerners before. He is paid more than Captain Chen. I am told that the barber is highly paid, too, but I have not used his services yet.

I am out of cigarettes. I ordered some from Kunming and they should be here in a day or so. I hope my clothes come, too.

I generally listen every night to "The Voice of Freedom," General MacArthur's station in the Philippines. It broadcasts the news at 5:30 p.m. our time on 9,650 kilocycles. The Japanese jam it so it is hard to understand. The hatred of the Japanese comes through loud and clear.

Olsen, Chennault and Sandel at Kunming.

Greenlaw, John Williams (head of AVG communications) and Chennault.

R. T. Smith in his P-40.

First Squadron ground personnel at Kunming after the battle of Rangoon. They are Neale, Locke (on plane), Musgrove, unidentified, Christensen, Blackburn, Harrington, Gove. Those kneeling are Kaelin, Curran, Cornelius, Kenner and Misenheimer. Pilot Mickelson is walking away.

First Squadron personnel. They are mostly ground crew.

The AVG bar on the second floor of Hostel One in Kunming. The one on the left is my friend, chess partner and AVG photographer J. H. (Pete) Pietsker. He sold me many of these photographs for $20 U.S. He told me that he was doing it as a favor since he had lost several rolls of film I had taken on the Burma Road. Later I discovered that most of the AVG had the same set of pictures.

March 10. *It's 6:20 p.m. and dinner won't be ready until about seven. I have not received a letter from home since the war started.*

The Burmese rupee has fallen from sixteen Chinese dollars to eight to one. Since we are paid in rupees, this means a fifty percent salary cut. However, as our principal items such as food, cigarettes, soap and razor blades are priced on the gold standard, it doesn't affect us too badly.

My room is heated with a small pot of glowing charcoal. There is no smoke, but I leave a window open a bit to let in fresh air and eliminate some of the fumes.

March 12. *Doreen Lonberg (now Doreen Reynolds) arrived yesterday noon by truck at my station which is on the main road to Chungking. My sedan parked in front has AVG painted on it in big letters. When she saw this she had the truck stop and let her off. She is engaged to Davis, who is on our staff in Kunming.*

Doreen had escaped from Hong Kong. She had been there during the siege and fall of the colony. Her stories tell of muddling and inefficiency. A friend of hers, Brian Fay, saw the first Japanese troops land on the island. He was one of the volunteers raised to defend the city. He rushed to the telephone and called military headquarters. He told them what he had seen. The officer on duty refused to tell the

The walled town of Cheng-Kung a few miles south of Kunming.

Chennault at Kunming. Walt Dolan took this obviously unposed picture.

A Chinese adobe house with a thatched roof. The woman at the door has bound feet.

Kunming after an air raid. This occurred shortly before the AVG moved from Burma to Kunming. The Japanese did not bomb Kunming while the AVG was stationed there. There were several bombing attacks later in 1943 and 1944, for I remember them vividly.

commanding general "for he was asleep." The British announced that all "British" women and children were removed from the colony. They did not include anyone with any Chinese blood. On the day the women were to register, many Eurasians possessing British passports thinking and looking like Englishmen, came to report. They were refused transportation. Yet the husbands of these women were volunteers in the Hong Kong forces. They were the best troops the city had. They spoke English and considered themselves British. One English woman of "pure" blood was told that she could be evacuated to Australia, but her three small children must remain behind. Her husband was part Chinese.

During the two and one-half week battle with the Japanese, the authorities refused to publish any casualty list since "it would be bad for morale." After the surrender, the British postal head asked the Japanese for their help in getting the names of the Hong Kong dead, many of them Eurasians. The Japanese agreed, but the British commanding officer refused to permit it; it still would "be bad for morale." Thousands of Hong Kong women did not know whether or not their husbands were dead.

"It wouldn't have been so bad, you see," Doreen said, "if they knew. Women can face it. But the uncertainty, the not knowing; some of them are mad with worry."

Dr. Lewis J. Richards. He never missed an AVG reunion.

One of the replacement P-40s at Kunming. The shark's teeth had not been painted on the nose of the plane.

Chennault planning a mission with the pilots of the First Squadron.

The engine overhaul area at Kunming. Bill Schaper was our chief mechanic in charge.

Hong Kong had 12,000 Canadian soldiers with two month's training. They were all young and inexperienced. Many of the officers of the Royal Scots were killed in a pillbox the first night of the battle. Although mobilized, they had no sentries and were engaged in a poker session. The Japanese threw a hand grenade into the cement building. Hong Kong had 4,000 volunteers, a goodly portion Eurasians. Their casualties were heavy.

Doreen escaped from Hong Kong through the aid of a German Nazi (who hated the Japanese), a Japanese officer, a Chinese patriot, members of the China Commando Group, the AVG and numerous other friends. She left Hong Kong on February 8, over a month ago. The first day she traveled by a Japanese boat. For five days she walked or rode in a sedan chair. Then she went by rail and truck to my station. She slept in beds with fleas, rats and other unmentionables. She ate any food she could find. She said she would have done it all again to get out of Hong Kong.

The Japanese are "horrible beasts." Two of her friends were raped and bayoneted and left for dead in their own blood. When sentries stopped her on the street, they felt her all over for "concealed weapons."

March 22. *I gave a talk the other night before a meeting of a local club in Kutsing. It is pronounced Shoe-shing. The audience was mostly Army officers and local government officials, all in uniforms or business suits. Mr. Chang, the hostel manager at Chanyi, translated for me. It is an odd sensation when the audience does not understand what you're saying. I would say a short paragraph and then stop, standing silently gazing at the faces of the audience, while Mr. Chang translated what I said. I would speak for three minutes, he for six. I think he padded my speech a bit. But then he knew what they wanted and knew more about the subject, "AVG," than I, for he has been with us for some time and is also a pilot.*

The Chinese are doing a fine job building new roads and factories to make radio tubes, transmitters, insulated rubber wire and so on. The railroad will soon be finished between here and Kutsing.

March 22. *It is about eight o'clock in the evening and I am in my room after dinner. I closed the station at six. It is raining—a nice warm rain. I am sipping a glass of good port from Portugal, have an American cigarette and a good book and I am as happy here as I could be anywhere.*

I find that we have many things in America that we do not need. They are nice to have, but it is the simple things that bring the most genuine pleasure. Good food, three friends who play bridge with me in the mornings, a bed in which I can always

The AVG staff at Toungoo. They are Wyke, Williams, Cedar, Adaj. Dr. Gentry, Chennault, Dr. Bruce, Greenlaw, Conant and Dr. Richards.

First Squadron personnel embarking at Kunming to fly to Kweilin.

Refueling Chennault's sedan.

R. M. Smith with the Chinese radiomen in front of the radio station at Cheng-Yi. Captain Chen Nan-Ning is to my left. The window is glazed with paper as we had no glass.

sleep and willing "boys" who keep the place clean, serve my meals, wash my car and run all errands—all this makes life very comfortable. Is it too luxurious? I guess it is if you consider that I am a soldier in the midst of the greatest war in history.

Yet it is a simple luxury not crowded with the motion picture theater, formal dinner parties, obligations to would-be friends, modern conveniences that require attention and other obligations. Here our contract bridge is played for pleasure by novices with no stakes.

A magazine printed in 1935 is just as welcome as the latest—only three or four months old. Everything in English is read slowly and deliberately and properly digested. The Book of Common Prayer, *five comedies of Shakespeare (in the 25¢ edition), an old edition of* The House of Seven Gables, The New China *written for Chinese middle school students studying English, a collection of English essays,* A Debate on Communism *with footnotes in Chinese, a copy of the* Atlantic *several months old, but very timely here, and a copy of* Robinson Crusoe *in Chinese and English represents a wealth of reading material. I often used to read two books a day and think nothing of it.*

Chief radio operator Lt. Chang in front of the radio station at Cheng-Yi.

Chinese radio operators and mechanics at Cheng-Yi. The Chinese characters on the Studebaker sedan read: Chinese Air Force, American Volunteer Group.

I may have to get down to smoking English cigarettes, as our stock of the American variety is low. The port is almost gone, too, but that is not a pressing problem. I enjoy it the more knowing it will soon be gone.

I do not mind the outside toilets and no plumbing—our ranch in Kansas had similar facilities. I don't get any letters, but then I do not have to answer any. The few I do write to my close friends and home are not an obligation. I know this is selfishness. But I have few alternatives, so I might as well enjoy it.

I played bridge this morning in the radio station while on duty. There was no activity on the net today. Captain Chen Nan-Ning, the officer in command of the Chinese attached to the station, and the two interpreters, Messrs. Li and Yeh, made the four. They are just learning the game, but I enjoyed it.

March 25. *Captain Chen told me an odd and amusing story today. He was down by the transmitter building and overheard two of our Yunnanese guards talking. One said, "Airplanes are wonderful, aren't they." The other replied, "Yes, they can get to India in one month." These soldiers are really young local boys from the farm. They have no idea of the speed of aircraft. A trip to India in the old days would take many months by pony caravan—perhaps even a year or two. To them one month was fast.*

Many of the local Chinese believe that they have an evil spirit following behind them. When they see a truck coming down the road at a fast clip, they will wait until the last minute, then dart across the road in front of the truck. Obviously, to them the evil spirit will then get killed. Unfortunately, the superstitious peasant is often killed instead. But this continues to happen.

March 26. *I heard today that we lost two pilots a few days ago in a strafing mission at Chiangmai in Thailand. John Newkirk, one of our top aces, was killed by gunfire from the ground. Bill McGarry was hit at the same time, but he was able to climb high enough to bail out. If he is alive, he is a prisoner. Johnny Fauth, a crew chief, was killed on the ground in a bombing raid at Magwe on March 22nd.*

April 10. *I received a Christmas card today from Sylvia, my brother Phil's fiancee. It was sent airmail on December 2. It was just a card signed "Sylvia." The postage was 70¢ American money.*

Al Probst, a pilot of the First Squadron, flew in yesterday in a P-40. He reported that ten AVG planes were strafed on the ground yesterday at Loiwing. The Japs came over at six in the morning. There was no warning since the warning net in Burma is a heliograph signaling machine, and it works only during sunny days. The Generalissimo and Madame Chiang Kai-shek were there with Colonel Chennault and got to see the fun. Fortunately the Japanese pilots' shooting was poor and little damage was done.

We keep hearing the question: "Where is the American Navy?" One rumor says it convoyed 500,000 troops to Australia. The British lost a carrier yesterday and two cruisers the day before in the Bay of Bengal.

Probst says that in Rangoon the British always had more Hurricanes than we had P-40s: "They didn't shoot down much, got four on their biggest day; we got twenty-six at the same time."

I found a copy today of Dale Carnegie's How To Win Friends and Influence People *in Chinese.*

April 11. *I still have not heard from my family since the war started. Some of the AVG have received airmail letters from home in three weeks. Perhaps some mail was lost in Rangoon or lost in India.*

I am going to give a dinner, Western style, for my Chinese staff. There will be twelve or more of them. Some of the young operators have never eaten with a knife and fork, so it will be fun. They laughed at me when I used chopsticks.

I am not learning as much Chinese as I would like to. I can tell the guard who I am, buy cigarettes in the market place and have learned most of the technical terms like "air raid," "aircraft," and so on. But I cannot carry on an extended conversation.

Captain Chen Nan-Ning (in the car) and Chinese radio personnel.

There is a story going around that the Philippine-Americans at Bataan wired Santa Barbara to hold out for thirty days and they would send reinforcements. We are amused at the air raid alerts on the West Coast of the United States.

Peanuts are plentiful here; they cost about twelve Chinese dollars for about two pounds. Pork is abundant, but beef is hard to get for the Chinese do not raise cattle for food. Chickens are cheap, and we have plenty of eggs.

I broke a spring on my car the other day in a chuckhole on the gravel road. The local auto mechanic fixed it in a novel but substantial way using some old clamps. The Chinese are very handy with tools.

April 12. *I went to the station this morning at six, started the engines, reported in to Boogie at Kunming and went back to bed. Mr. Chang, the hostel manager, was at the station the other day and noticed that I was sleepy after lunch. He had a cot brought to the station and installed near the receivers. So I get up, drive three miles, open the station and go to bed again!*

There is a Chinese operator on duty and will wake me up if he hears our call letters or my name. I returned to the hostel about eight o'clock for a breakfast of ham, eggs, toast, hot cakes and coffee. I then returned to the station and read until noon. I am reading Barchester Towers by Anthony Trollope.

After lunch I played bridge with Larry Tu, Captain Chen and Mr. Li. I came back to the hostel at 7 p.m. for dinner, finished the book, and in a few minutes I shall go to bed. This has been an average day.

John Briggs, an English Red Cross man at Kutsing, picked up a dying Chinese soldier on the road the other day and took him to the local hospital. As the soldier died, John was told by the local magistrate that he must pay the burial expenses. According to local custom, he is responsible. He should not have touched the soldier. The proper procedure would be for John to call the local police. The police would report the death to the army, which would either send for the soldier or tell the hospital to send for him. In China if you save a person's life, you become responsible for that person.

John probably will not have to pay, since Dr. Lai, the chief doctor at the hospital, is a good friend of his. Dr. Lai is giving the Kutsing magistrate free shots for syphilis.

April 17. *It is very quiet here. There is little action at Chanyi. I hear the other end of the net, Lashio and Loiwing, talking to planes, giving their pilots the latest reports of enemy activity and talking of air alerts. The radiomen use the Chinese words "JING BOW" for air raid. They talk of scores of ten to one in our favor. Shreffler is at BL-4 now at Loiwing, where he went from Chanyi. I hear his voice every day telling of enemy planes shot down near him and giving instructions to our planes.*

But here nothing happens. From 0530 to 1800 I am on watch with time off for breakfast and lunch. I read Dostoevski, Tolstoi, Wodehouse, Shakespeare and anything I can find. I even study debates on capitalism, communism and socialism with Chinese footnotes.

The Burma Road winds around the hill below our station. I can stand on our balcony and see the trucks filled with gasoline; soldiers and boxes of war supplies pass on their way to Chungking. There are not so many now, for the shortage of gasoline is acute. The Chinese are converting their trucks so that they may run on charcoal.

But if there are fewer trucks now on the road, there are more two-wheel wooden carts, pulled by tough little ponies, yellow cows or great lumbering water buffaloes. Fifty-five gallon drums of gasoline are hauled on these small carts. Coolies trot by carrying charcoal, lumber and odd looking bundles in wicker-work packs. Soldiers march by on their 2,000 kilometer walk to the Burma front. Sometimes they have a dog on a leash that will be a future meal. The wounded, sick or discouraged drop by the wayside to get better or die.

Francis Muir, speaking from Delhi in India to the Columbia Broadcasting Company in America, said that the United States Army in India had no coffee or American cigarettes. I do have coffee here, but cigarettes are all gone. I buy Cotabs from the market place. They are smuggled in from Indo-China and cost thirteen dollars Chinese for a package of twenty. They are not bad. I like them better than the English Gold Flakes or Players. English cigarettes cost twenty-two Chinese dollars for a pack of ten. If one can find American cigarettes they are priced at sixty dollars to eighty dollars a pack. Since the Chinese dollar is worth about two cents in American money, or as people say in the Far East "gold," the prices aren't too bad for native brands. Indian rupees are 9.5 to 1 for American dollars now on the black market.

April 20. *Li and Tu, the two interpreters, are planning two one-act plays, both in two languages. I made the mistake of telling them of our annual Spanish Fiesta of high school days in the Simi Valley in southern California—how it was always in both English and Spanish in that agricultural community with a large Mexican population. Now I am to have a role in each of their plays. Li's is original, but Tu is making a steal from Mansfield. Instead of Norse characters they will be Chinese, Burmese and American. The scene is the enemy side of the Burma front. I play the part of an AVG pilot who is hidden in "The Locked Chest."*

Sidney Bailey, an English Red Cross volunteer, tells me "you call it English." He is firmly convinced that Americans have their own language and that the dialect spoken in England is the pure form. Of course I remind him that we have no cockney or Oxford accent. I also quoted some Englishman who said that "educated

Scotsmen or Americans make the best radio announcers." He told me of a sign in a Swiss hotel: "English spoken, American understood."

April 21. *It is a bit cool this morning. Yesterday I had a charcoal fire in a pot at the station, but today I wore an extra sweater under my flight jacket. It is clear and warm in the sun. In India it is over 100 degrees Fahrenheit. The 6,000 foot altitude makes the climate quite pleasant.*

I cleaned the transmitter the other day and found a mouse in it! I went to the transmitter shack about a half a mile away and when I turned on the plate current the mouse squealed! I opened the side panel and chased it out.

8:00 p.m. I finished the detective story omnibus this afternoon and started on Voltaire's Zodig. *I wonder if I can sleep if I go to bed.*

I tuned into the Japanese radio stations today. They have a regular English broadcast. They were lamenting the first bombing of Japan. The damage must have been considerable for the announcer spent so much time denying it. None of the Japanese stories agreed. Hong Kong reported ninety American planes, all B-17s. Tokyo said there were twelve or fifteen B-25s in the raid. They said that nothing was hit except schools and hospitals, and plenty of those. One announcer spent five minutes talking about the poor, innocent children. The Japanese did not talk of that when they bombed China. Their propaganda is very crude. British propaganda is better, but American is the best for we stick more closely to the truth and are always so comfortably optimistic.

The other night I played a part in the one-act show written by John Mansfield and translated and adapted to a Burmese setting by Larry Tu. He did a good job and the play contained much action. There was a Burmese traitor, a loyalist Chinese wife played by Captain Chen's wife, four Japanese soldiers and one "forced down" AVG pilot played by me. It was, of course, all in Chinese, and I had to practice the tones a lot. But it was hard for me, although my lines were short and there were not very many of them. I was supposed to be sarcastic in Chinese. The audience consisted of about 500 Yunnanese and the central government officers. They seemed to like it. I asked Captain Chen how they liked my Chinese. He said that they thought it was excellent but that I probably spoke another dialect!

April 22. *Cliff Groh, an AVG pilot, is missing. No one knows where he is, as he had no radio in his P-40. He may have landed in some out-of-the-way place.*

I see the boy is bringing my dinner to the dining room next door and he will soon be here to say, "Dinner all ready, sir." He carries it 100 yards from the kitchen, yet it is always hot. The food is generally very good, but we have run out of butter. Butter is imported, generally from Australia, and is not made or eaten by the Chinese. Some missionaries will make it if they have a cow.

The main gate of the walled town of Cheng-Yi. The gate was of heavy iron and closed at night. Standing beside R. M. Smith is a British soldier who had escaped from Burma and Marlin R. (Bud) Hubler.

Sidney Bailey gave me some peanut butter that he had made. It is very good and a reasonable substitute for butter. The local markets have lots of peanuts.

April 28. *John Blackburn was killed in Kunming today. It was an accident. He was testing his guns over the lake and failed to pull out of a dive.*

April 29. *It is cloudy and has been rainy for the past few days. The weather makes me feel sad and despondent. I am a bit chilly and feel at odds with the world and bored. My mother, who is a registered nurse, would suggest a physic, the guys in Kunming a drink. I have no physic, so I will have a glass of brandy tonight.*

The AVG got thirteen enemy planes yesterday according to Ed Lussier, the radio operator at BL-4. However, our communiqué as read by the Chinese radio station in Chungking said eleven. Japanese planes bombed our field for I heard instructions to the pilots warning them of "termite holes." The enemy planes shot down were Zeros. We did not lose any planes.

Lashio is being evacuated, and so is Loiwing from the scraps of information I pick up on our frequency. London or Chungking has not announced it, yet rumor says that the Japanese soldiers are near Lashio, having come in around the flank of the Chinese armies from Thailand. Our radio station left Lashio the other day.

Yesterday the Japanese fliers were on our frequency, six thousand forty-eight kilocycles. One of our pilots used some profane language and told one of them to get off. The Japanese pilot came on our frequency with "so sorry." The enemy listens to everything we say. I hope they have a difficult time understanding our slang.

May 1. *I heard on our net that BL-4 at Loiwing is moving out today. I do not know whether it is due to the start of the rainy season or because the Japanese have come so close to the field. Some American transports are helping in the move. These United States planes have been carrying supplies to Yunnanyi, even gasoline. Frank Schwartz died in Poona, India on April 24.*

May 2. *Our radio station, BL-4 and all AVG personnel left Loiwing due to the proximity of the Japanese troops.*

May 3. *A rumor has reached here that the Japanese are at the Yunnan border on the Burma Road. Yesterday nine of our P-40s bombed Lashio and hit the airport there. India's congress adopted "passive resistance" to the Japanese. American war ships are in the Mediterranean, which does not help out here. All of the news seems black and the war promises to be a lengthy affair. The British talk of the bravery (in retreat) of their armies in Burma. London radio is always saying that*

England owes much to them. But from the stories of their action coming to us from the front, it seems more like a big defeat to me.

6:40 p.m. It is raining. I guess the rainy season has started. I hope it will hold up the Japanese; nothing else seems to. There is heavy thunder and lightning, causing my telephone to ring. The switchboard operator refuses to answer if one calls during a storm. Or if he does it is to say, in Chinese, that he won't make any connections until it stops thundering. As the Chinese would say, "May yo fa tze"—it can't be helped.

We have started a garden at the station. Six soldiers, an interpreter, Captain Chen and I are digging in it. We have some flower seeds, corn and beans and are looking for tomato seeds. We are talking about a summer house or a small pagoda to play bridge in. We are looking for trees to transplant. I wish I had a dollar's worth of American seeds. Most of the Chinese eat two meals a day; the interpreters eat three. The first meal is around nine in the morning and the second in the afternoon at four o'clock. Judging from the large amounts of rice consumed at a sitting, they do not lose much by eating only twice.

These two meals a day caused some problems in Kunming. I had eight or nine carpenters working in the warehouse building an office and shelves. They were paid twenty-five Chinese dollars a day, good by their wage scales. But they never appeared in the morning until after 9:30 a.m. and left before four in the afternoon. They would say, "Chee fan, chee fan," which means literally "eat rice." I always suspected that they had another job as well as ours. They have improved on the eight-hour day.

These carpenters were very slow. However, they had to make every piece of the lumber they used out of rough logs and planks. The result was very good; the doors were attractive. They used very few nails and probably could have done without them except that I furnished them free. Their tools were primitive and in some cases made by themselves.

The Chinese are a cheerful people, generally very natural in their habits. They like to laugh. They generally avoid physical exercise, although the young people like basketball and other milder games. They like to eat, to make love, to go to their theater, to talk and to make money. The differences between our peoples are customs and manners. Their moral code is different from ours.

May 4. *Yesterday Paoshan was bombed by fifty-one Japanese bombers, two waves of twenty-seven and twenty-four. There was no warning. Our net has completely broken down along the Burmese border. Our planes were caught on the ground. A few were damaged but not seriously, for the Japanese missed the field with bombs and then strafed it with model Os or Zeros. Charlie Bond was shot down but he bailed out and was not hurt. The loss of life in the walled city of Paoshan must have* *been terrible. There were many refugees from Burma there.*

Early this morning a report came over our net that Wanting was lost. The Japanese are making better time up the road than we did in convoy.

9:00 p.m. A report came in this evening that the Japanese are only fifty kilometers from Paoshan. The bridge over the Salween River is reported cut and fierce fighting is going on around it. Ed Lussier, our radioman who has been retreating one step ahead of the advancing Japanese for the four months, reached the AVG station BC-5 at Paoshan today. He was at Toungoo, Rangoon, Magwe, Lashio, Loiwing and Wanting and with Bob King operated the radio station from a truck. They always brought their radio equipment with them. Bob and Ed have been among the last to leave at almost everyone of the AVG fields. Tonight Ed called BG-8 at Kunming and requested permission to remain at BC-5. He said that he had to fight his way up the road and used his tommy gun on some Japanese in order to get through. He said he wanted another crack at the bastards.

May 5. *This morning BG-8 at Kunming was unable to raise BC-5. The Chinese report that their Paoshan station does not answer. Late reports last night said the Japanese were a few miles from the city. Sasser, the AVG radioman at BC-5, had requested permission to evacuate Paoshan. Apparently he has done so. The enemy's advance up the Burma Road has been extraordinary.*

I requested a tommy gun from Kunming. I do not have a pistol. We are not sure of the loyalty of the Yunnanese troops.

Their leader is called "the old tiger" or Lao Lung Yun and is an old time war lord who has been very independent of the central government in the past. Captain Chen says that the AVG does not have to worry about the Yunnanese, for they like us due to the lack of air raids while we have been here. I am not so sure. The Yunnanese and the central troops had a small battle in Kunming about two months ago. They used rifles, hand grenades and machine guns. The Yunnanese detachment was just about wiped out. We did have local troops guarding this hostel, but now a platoon of central troops have taken over. Hopefully I will not be murdered in my bed. The receiving station and the transmitter that is about a half mile away are guarded by Yunnanese troops.

Noon. I just received orders to send Captain Chen to Kunming for some important job. I will sure miss him, for he knows more about the station than I do. I consider him a friend—and he plays bridge!

7:00 p.m. I just received word that Larry Tu is to go to Kunming immediately. That knocks out our bridge foursome completely. Radiograms were sent by our headquarters to all radio station masters offering them technical sergeant. The consensus was a definite no. We all want to go home.

May 6. *Generally we close the AVG radio net at sundown. Sometimes when Japa-*

nese activity is suspected, we keep it open at night with Chinese radio operators. We do not let them use voice but change frequencies and have them use a key and Morse code. Like radio operators everywhere, they like to gossip. But how do you do it in Chinese? Chinese has thousands of characters—one needs at least three thousand to read a newspaper. The Chinese have developed a code book, with a number of five digits assigned to each character. To use the code, one has to look up the number and transmit it, and the other station has to look it up, too. Obviously, this takes forever and is impractical for casual conversation. Besides, we do not have a copy of the code book. So the Chinese operators use English. They are all high school graduates and have studied English for years. They are very weak in conversation, but they can read fairly well. I find pages of scratch paper with their notes when I relieve them in the morning. They are breaking some rules, but I haven't said anything. It's a boring job to sit by a radio receiver all night just listening to it crackle.

8:00 p.m. I feel really proud of myself! I cured Lt. Chang's athlete's foot! About a week ago he was limping around in his slippers and in pain. I asked him about it, and he showed me his feet. They were red and swollen, the worst case of infection I had ever seen. A couple of years ago I had read of a cure for syphilis. The doctors increased the heat in a patient's body, keeping the head and brain cool for several hours. This killed the germs but did not harm the body, for it can adjust to gradually increasing heat. The amount of increase in temperature did not have to be more than a few degrees, just enough to kill the virus but not the patient.

I had him put his feet in a pan of rather warm water. We kept a tea kettle boiling over a pot of burning charcoal and I gradually and carefully added hot water to the wash basin. This raised the temperature of the water. His feet adjusted to it; it did not feel too hot for him. We did this for four times a day for a week. It killed the fungus and his feet look fine. I had him boil his socks and wash out his shoes with a little gasoline. It did not hurt my reputation with the station staff.

May 7. *Larry Tu was sent to Kunming this morning. Li, the other interpreter, is teaching school in the village, so Chang and I have to struggle along as best we can. He has about six English words, one of them "okay." My Chinese is weak, so we use a lot of sign language. Chang is the telephone operator for the air raid warning net. His room with the telephones is right next to my receiver room. He feeds me all the information of aerial activity in Yunnan Province.*

May 8. *I heard today that Ben Foshee was killed in Paoshan on May 4.*

May 9. *There is more news on the radio of the naval battle near the Coral Sea this morning. Seventeen Japanese ships were sunk, including two carriers. I hope this* *is the battle we have been hoping for. BBC in London said it may be the largest battle in naval history.*

May 10. *Roger Shreffler, Captain Chen and his wife, Bill Sykes and Francis Doran came here last night on the way to establish an AVG radio station in Chungking. An English RAF radioman named Jepson who is attached to the AVG was with them. Shreffler and the Chens did not get here until two in the morning due to car trouble in Kunming.*

Bill and I and the two others ate a leisurely dinner and drank some cognac. They told stories of their retreat from Rangoon through Toungoo, Magwe, Lashio, Loiwing and Paoshan. Manning Wakefield and Joe Sweeney, a radioman, shot down one Japanese plane from the ground with tommy guns. They both got caught near the field while the Japs were strafing and fired at the enemy planes until one crashed. One of the tommy gun slugs was found in a Japanese pilot's head.

Later Sweeney got caught on the field when the Japanese were dropping big bombs. There was no ditch, no hole. He was riding in a jeep at the time. He jumped out of the jeep and let it run off in gear. A minute later a bomb hit it. Sweeney lay flat on the ground and every time a bomb hit the field he bounced! Luckily he was not hit; his only wound was mental—his feelings were hurt.

May 11. *Yesterday Shreffler told me about Johnny Fauth's death at Magwe. During a bomb raid an Australian sergeant pilot had made a crash landing on the field. Olie, "the little mech" (Henry Olson), and Fauth ran out to the plane to get the pilot out. He was out of his head; the ship was full of Prestone fumes and on fire. They dragged him out of the cockpit as he was fighting and yelling and got him over to the trench.*

Then they decided to go over and put out the fire. While they were working the fire extinguisher, the Japanese plane came over strafing. Olson was not touched, but Fauth was hit yet still able to walk. Olie got him over to the trench again and then had to leave to help Schwartz, an AVG pilot that had been hit near the field. Olie got in a jeep and in a few minutes a bomb hit near it and threw it up in the air. All the clothes and personal gear that Olie had stored in the jeep were completely destroyed. He flew out and slid for thirty feet on the seat of his pants down the runway, but he wasn't hurt. He then got a sedan, picked up Schwartz and went back to get Fauth.

Fauth was in the back seat in pretty bad condition. Japanese bombers were over the field again, dropping more bombs. Shrapnel hit the glass of the car breaking the windows. Fauth told Olie he was a damned fool to try to drive to the hospital during the raid and kept repeating that he ought to get in a ditch. At the hospital Dr. Richards, one of our doctors and a damned good one, worked on Schwartz and

Fauth, but Fauth was in serious condition. He knew he was dying. He asked Olie to pay Engle thirty rupees that he owed him, to write his parents and to take care of his things. He died about two in the morning. He was a good man. He was the only member of the ground crew that we have lost so far.

There are no prisoners taken on the Burma front. General Stilwell had to offer a 1,000 rupees reward to get one Japanese soldier. When his troops did get the prisoner, he was so badly beaten up that they had to wait several days to question him. He told them that the Japanese did not take prisoners either.

Some of our pilots ate breakfast with General Stilwell recently and brought back the story and explanation of the Japanese breakthrough and the loss of Lashio. The British retreated and left a thirty mile hole in the center of our lines. Stilwell did not know it. They refuse to give any information to the Americans or Chinese.

I write this on duty. Several Japanese observation planes and perhaps some bombers are over Yunnan. AVG so far has all three squadrons in the air. Reports from my radio net are coming in a steady stream. Planes call this and other stations in the net. New planes are also over Yunnan, being ferried from Calcutta, and they are calling, asking for their positions.

One CNAC plane called BG-8, our net control station in Kunming, while American transports ask about the enemy position. A station in Calcutta, CGO, asks for the weather. Peltsker, who is at the hostel, calls on the telephone to ask if the jing bow is urgent. The Chinese telephone operator takes reports. Chief operator Chang and Yeu search maps spread on tables and walls for the towns reporting the enemy. They give me the sector, and I report to Kunming. Our frequency is cluttered and crowded.

We have five or six telephones with a direct line to the Chinese central net control radio station here. There is a telephone line north that ties in with the air warning net section in northern Yunnan. There are also other direct lines that I use—one to the transmitter and engine room where a Yunnanese soldier is on duty twenty-four hours a day and another line to my room in the hostel. Sometimes the phones ring almost constantly. I generally guard only one frequency, although I have three receivers. Boogie at BG-8 guards five frequencies. He is one of the best radio operators I have ever known.

May 13. *There is much discussion about the future of the AVG. July 4 is induction day, with strings attached. Wally Jordan, an AVG weatherman, is supposed to come in tonight with a convoy. It is almost 7:00 p.m., and there is no sign of him. He is bringing a spring for my car, cigarettes, pay and, I hope, reading material.*

I had Li spend the day checking AVG gasoline stores in the district. We have about 1,000 gallons left for this station.

May 16. *I heard a story that seems hard to believe. Some of the AVG ground men were drinking in Kunming with two Army Air Force pilots, both second lieutenants. The pilots had just flown in with a load of gas on a C-47. Our men were bemoaning the fact that we did not have any bombers, arguing that it would be much more efficient to bomb Hanoi, destroying the Japanese planes on the ground, than to shoot them down one by one in the air. Nearly everyone in the AVG is always crying for bombers, from Chennault on down.*

About midnight, when everyone was feeling pretty good, one of the American pilots said, "I could bomb Hanoi with my C-47." One of the AVG ground men had the keys to the bomb storage bunkers near the field and replied, "I've got the bombs." Someone said, "Let's go," and they did. They took off about one in the morning and got over Hanoi about three o'clock. The city was brightly lit, since it had never been hit with an air raid at night by the Chinese. They pushed the bombs out through the side cargo door of the plane. One of the AVG almost went with the bombs. They turned around and headed back to Kunming. They were lost for a while but finally landed at the airport about eight in the morning. By that time they were cold sober and tired. They said nothing to anyone but went to the hostel and to bed. The next morning Chinese intelligence congratulated Colonel Chennault on the first successful night bombing of Hanoi. Intelligence reported that a Japanese general was killed in the raid and that Hanoi would have to black out at night hereafter.

The courtyard of the hostel where I lived in Cheng-Yi.

May 17. *Ed Lussier came through the other day on his way to eastern China. He will drive over 2,000 kilometers to install a new AVG radio station out there. After we leave it will be taken over by the United States Army Air Corps. Miller is following him to install another in the same province. The call letters have been assigned for five AVG stations in the east, WC-l, WC-2 and so on. Someone has a sense of humor for WC is British slang for water closet, which is British for toilet. My station call letters are BO-2.*

There is a rumor of a Japanese thrust into eastern China.

Ed had to fight his way up the road from Lashio and Loiwing. Some of the Yunnanese troops went over to the enemy. Ed carried a tommy gun. He directed traffic near the Paoshan road that was jammed after a bomb raid. He said that ten thousand people were killed in Paoshan. All but two bombs from fifty-one Japanese bombers hit within the city walls. The gutters were full of blood, trucks drove over bodies and there was widespread panic. The Chinese soldiers were retreating from the Japs. The AVG planes came in and bombed and strafed the enemy. The Chinese attacked and stopped them. The Japanese lost thousands of troops.

Tom Jones was killed yesterday at Kunming. He was practicing a bomb run. The belly tank had been taken off the P-40 and a bomb attached instead. The bomb exploded too soon.

Today Lewis Bishop bailed out over Japanese lines while returning from another bombing raid on Hanoi. The Chinese radio net said that he was all right but in enemy territory. Only yesterday Bishop landed here in a P-40 and ate lunch with me. He brought up a generator for Shreffler's truck. Shreffler is going to Chungking to establish a radio station there.

Yesterday's AVG mission destroyed fifteen Japanese planes on the ground and probably damaged thirty more. Our planes dropped bombs and strafed. I have not heard any reports from today's mission.

Miller came through last night. One jeep turned over on the road, one of his Chinese radio operators was killed and another has a brain concussion. I had heard that Miller had turned over his truck, ruining his radio equipment, but it was not true. I sent a truck down the road to check on his condition.

May 17. *Our hostel is becoming a busy place. Bill Schaper came in day before yesterday with a convoy of three jeeps and eleven International trucks headed for Chungking. His drivers are English soldiers who escaped from Burma. Schaper got an early start yesterday but had a generator burn out on the truck and came back to Chanyi in a jeep. He sent the convoy on to Annam. I called Kunming and asked to have another generator flown up.*

Bill told me a lot about the evacuation of Rangoon. His was the last convoy to leave the city and had to detour to the east to avoid Japanese troops. In January he volunteered to go to Rangoon. Since he is in charge of group engineering and one of our best mechanics, he was needed there. I asked him why he went down to Burma. "They were my ships," he said. "I wanted to be with my ships."

He really gets bitter if a mechanic or pilot has a stupid accident and damages one of "his" ships.

Four other mechanics volunteered to go with Schaper. They were Irving Gove, Ed McClure, Dick Graham and John Uebele. They flew down to Lashio in the Beechcraft with Bill in the co-pilot's seat. The pilot was Moon Chin, Chennault's personal pilot. The radio was out and they knew they wouldn't have any warning of Japanese planes. Lashio was a mess—there was no place to eat in the town. They took off for Toungoo and caught the train there for Rangoon. It took them over fourteen hours to go about two hundred miles. They almost starved for the railroad station dining rooms were out of food. They did get bread and butter at one stop. They had one can of pork and beans with some catchup for breakfast divided five ways.

Before the British evacuated Rangoon, they burned the supplies on the docks. Over 400 brand new trucks were burned. They could have been loaded with gasoline and supplies and sent up the road to China, but there was no organization. Everyone of our men got a jeep to drive. Before the supplies were destroyed, everyone helped himself to gin, shotgun shells, radios, bolts of cloth, perfume, shoe polish and any thing else of value. The goods would have been worth a fortune in China.

Most of the physical work in Burma was done by imported Indians. When the bombs started to fall, they left. The Chinese owned most of the shops, the British ran the government and the Burmese became monks and wore yellow robes.

On February 22 the British let the lepers and insane out of the asylums and prisons. Rangoon was in flames. Schaper and his convoy left the next day, heading for the airfield at Magwe in central Burma. Many of the trucks were driven by RAF enlisted men. Some of the trucks towed jeeps; some jeeps had another jeep dragging from the rear. Schaper had a dismantled airplane in his International truck— a Stinson-105 that had belonged to U Saw, the Burmese leader. The trucks were loaded with spare parts for the P-40s, ammunition, and much loot picked up from the Rangoon docks. They had two Studebaker gas trucks driven by RAF men. Paul Frillman, our chaplain, led another convoy loaded with miscellaneous supplies and many cases of whiskey. He also had about twenty Eurasian girls that had been quite friendly with the members of the AVG.

Many of the shopkeepers gave their keys to the AVG when they left Rangoon. "Take what you want and then burn it," they said.

When Bill left Rangoon there were only nine pilots and their P-40s remaining in the city. Bob Neale and Snuffy Smith were the last to fly out on February 28, retreating to the field at Magwe. Rangoon fell to the Japanese ground troops on

March 1. All of the loot was carried on one truck. In an accident on the Burma Road this truck and all of its cargo was completely destroyed.

May 18. *It is amusing to watch the Chinese radio operators play cards. They have watched me play solitaire during the long hours on watch and now play themselves and are quicker to see plays than I am. One operator whom I call "Dopey" has a tendency to cheat! Two of them were playing two-handed bridge this evening; although they speak very little English, they bid "two hearts," "three spades" and so on. If they go set, they say "one down."*

I find that they learn English and particularly "American" faster than I learn Chinese. I have learned their expressions they use most and especially the words connected with aircraft, our warning net and the AVG. Chinese is a perfect language in some respects since it has no grammar, no singular, no plural and no declensions with past, present or future and is monosyllabic. It does have four tones, but one of them may be indicated by our question mark and another by an explanation point.

British trucks, mostly empty except for gasoline, and driven by Englishmen, are passing daily, escaping from Burma. Thirty or forty a day have gone by for the past few weeks. Most of the trucks are American made.

London radio broadcasts talk of the heroic British soldiers in their withdrawal from Burma. They put their shoulders to the wheel to get the trucks out of mud holes. BBC seems to be proud that the Japanese cannot keep up with them. Yet the Chinese are dying in Burma in a desperate fight against the Japanese. The Chinese live on a handful of rice a day, are shod in straw sandals, have no trucks and little mechanical equipment. Even their supply of guns is limited. I know, for I have seen them pass here on the way to the front. They are ill clad and poorly paid, have little food and are walking down to Burma. The British are taking empty trucks the other way.

May 19. *Today Francis Lee and Irene Vincent stopped and talked for an hour or so with me at the station. I was daydreaming in front of the crackling receiver when I heard a knock on the door. This startled me, for the Chinese never knock; they just come in. I opened the door, and there stood a beautiful American young woman with long blonde hair. I thought I was dreaming. I stammered something, then invited them in.*

Lee is a press correspondent for the International News Service and is writing a story on the AVG communications for an American newspaper. Miss Vincent is with the Red Cross. They told more stories of the fall of Hong Kong. British soldiers who have escaped say that it was one of the blackest spots in the history of the British Empire. Incredible stupidity and mismanagement were evident in the com-

mand structure. The governor's chief concern, and he had many a heated debate about it, was whether or not his secretary should wear blue silk lapels. The secretary of the king does, and as a representative of the king, the governor should also wear them, this was his argument. All this was going on between the eighth of December and the fall of Hong Kong. A British newspaper man is reported to have remarked to the governor, "This, I suppose, is what the Russians are fighting for."

It is cold today and there is a little rain. It is completely overcast. The rainy season is starting by easy stages and not with a bang as I had expected. I am wearing two wool sweaters and a lined leather flight jacket with a fur collar, and I am still cold.

Captain Hemingway of the British military mission came in tonight on his way to Chentu. He is a capital fellow and has been thirty years in China. We talked of the war and of his early days in China. He has been in Inner Mongolia. He made several trips taking gasoline across the desert for Eurasian Airlines so that the planes could refuel when they made the long trip. The gasoline went by train, then in pony carts and finally on camels. A camel could carry sixteen tins of petrol.

May 22. *Robert Little was killed near the Salween River today.*

May 25. *Francis Lee, the INS correspondent, came back again last night. He had gotten as far as Pingyi, forty kilometers from here, and stayed there five days. He left Pingyi seven times for Chungking. He had a high pressure leak in a tire that never got fixed, he had a broken gear box and several other breakdowns. He would start out, something would happen and he would return. The natives got to know the car quite well; it was called "the car that is going to Chungking." It furnished a week's amusement for the village. Francis Lee speaks Chinese quite well. He says that the AVG will be remembered in Chinese history as we remember LaFayette and the other volunteers of 1776. He said that the most encouraging thing he noticed was that the AVG gets along so well with the Chinese. He thinks that our relationship is amazing.*

We could not have accomplished what we have without the Chinese. They not only feed us and provide a marvelous air raid warning net, but they also support us in so many other ways.

Eighteen or so of the RAF have been with the AVG since the fall of Rangoon. They are good lads, but they take an awful beating. Every time the British have a defeat they hear about it. The AVG has really put them to work as auto mechanics, gas truck drivers and so on. The English seem to be happy with us and proud of our victories.

The AVG radio station masters have been offered master sergeant if they will re-enlist in the American Army Air Corps on July 4. Most of them are declining.

May 25. *Today Bob King, AVG radioman at Kunming, said that Richardson might relieve me for a few days so that I can go to headquarters and see the sights. I have been here almost three months with no day off. I am out of books, magazines and newspapers. Rupees have hit a new low on the black market; they are five and one-half Chinese dollars for one rupee. We used to get fifteen or sixteen to one rupee. There is no demand now for Burmese rupees since Burma is lost and the smugglers have no use for them.*

We have lost four pilots in the last week. John Donovan was bombing Hanoi in a P-40E and ground fire hit his plane. He crashed and was killed instantly. The next day Tom Jones crashed while practicing dropping bombs near Kunming. Bishop had to bail out while returning from another bombing of Hanoi. The French officials had him; he was all right but the Japanese took him over. Rumors say that the Generalissimo offered a huge ransom for him. Then we lost another pilot on a raid on the Japanese troops in Yunnan. I heard BB-1, our AVG station in Yunnanyi, say the other night, "Eight left; seven came back."

Bob Little was killed on May 22 in a bombing raid on Jap troops near the Salween. He was hit by ground fire. He was a double ace, with over ten enemy planes to his credit.

When the Japanese do not come over to us, we carry the war to them. But it is very expensive. The pilots we lose are almost always the bravest, most popular fellows in the AVG. We have lost only two or three in actual combat with the Japanese but too many in accidents. We have destroyed between 300 and 400 Japanese planes.

Cliff Groh is still missing. He got lost near Tibet. He left his plane and started to walk to civilization. He will probably show up after the war.

May 27. *I found an old American magazine dated November, 1938. I do not mind reading a continued story starting in the middle, but when it says "continued in the next issue," I am disgusted. There is no chance of finding the next issue around here.*

May 28. *Life is too easy here. My meals are always hot, efficiently served and very good. I throw my soiled clothes on the floor; the boy takes them away and brings them back nice and clean and puts them away in the proper drawer. While I eat lunch or breakfast, two or three of the Chinese servants clean my car. The mechanics keep the tank full of gas and check the oil and water and look for odd squeaks. I check and clean the transmitter once a month. Between these checks I seldom see it. The power engine needs a few minutes of attention a day.*

The moon is almost full tonight. I wandered out of my courtyard to the edge of the hill and gazed at the valley of Chanyi below. The white pale radiance glistened on the flooded rice paddies that terraced the hills. In the distance the mountains of

Yunnan were outlined against the Chinese summer sky. The Burma Road was a pale yellow ribbon that ran up the valley, past the walled town and into the northern hills. There are no lights visible in the town tonight. Chanyi has not changed even though China's main highway runs by its door. Behind the rough stone walls and medieval gates of heavy iron, the Yunnanese eat, live and die in the same way their forebears did in the time of Aristotle. Women with tiny bound feet carry water from the nearby spring, coolies in wide straw hats jog by, swinging their load on a yo-yo pole and ancient men sit in the sun engaged in hunting for an occasional louse.

But change will come. Every truck that passes the west gate brings to Chanyi a current from the outside world. Already there is a radio station in the temple. Yunnan crones look, with an air of stolid indifference, at electric lights, where a few months ago were fluttering oil lamps illuminating a Buddhist altar.

As I stood there tonight on the hillside, watching the moonlight on the turreted walls and towers of this ancient town, I wondered when the local citizens would build a service station at the west gate. I could see a sign advertising hamburgers.

June 2. *Chungking announced on the radio today that the AVG is being reorganized July 4. It will no longer be the American Volunteer Group of the Chinese Air Force but the U.S. Army Air Corps' 23rd Pursuit Group. It did not announce that most of us will not stay. Rumor says that all radiomen will get commissions.*

June 25. *Bruce, a sergeant just in from the United States, came up last night to relieve me and tomorrow I am going to Kunming. I have been offered a commission as second lieutenant. But I am going home.*

This picture was taken by AVG pilot Robert T. Smith, who holds the copyright. Reprinted by permission of R. T. Smith.

3

The Air Raid Warning Net

Early warnings of enemy activity have always been necessary for people defending their homes and cities. In ancient times every walled city had watchtowers. Lookouts were stationed on surrounding hills to warn of approaching soldiers. A system of signal fires was common in the days before electronic communications. In England at the time of the Spanish Armada, picket boats were stationed offshore to guard against surprise. Knowledge of the location of the enemy is highly important in planning both the defense and counterattack.

When airplanes were developed that flew about 200 miles an hour, early warning became more imperative. Aircraft precisely lined up in straight lines on the ground provide an excellent target for any enemy. A timely intelligence of approaching fighters or bombers is the difference between victory and defeat. Since the speed of the approaching enemy is so much faster than that of horses or marching men, observers must be many miles away to be effective. A system of communications must be developed to get the information to ground commanders and the pilots in the air.

The incredible fact is that this simple and basic concept was so late in being developed. In the Philippines General MacArthur's aircraft were mostly destroyed on the ground. There was no semblance of an air raid warning system. In addition, the planes were lined up in a military straight row in keeping with the belief this would make protection from sabotage easier.

If there had been a good air raid warning system in the Philippines our forces there could have held out for many more months. A few planes with determined pilots commanded by an intelligent and knowledgeable leader can strike at key enemy concentrations with devastating effect. For example, a few P-40s flown by our brave and skillful pilots were instrumental in stopping the Japanese thrust into

Yunnan at the Salween River in early 1942. If it had not been for this swift and successful attack, the Japanese would have overrun Yunnan Province, knocking China out of the war.

General Chennault was well aware of the basic necessity of an early warning system. He began to promote the idea to the Chinese when he first went to China in 1937. When the first nets were developed in eastern China, it soon became apparent that they had other very important advantages. First, they gave warning to the people in the cities that a raid was imminent. The people had time to leave the target areas and go to the countryside or to find trenches for protection. A system of notification to the populace was devised whereby one large black paper ball was hoisted on a flag pole when the enemy planes were about one hour away. A two-ball signal meant they were thirty minutes from the city. Three balls indicated that they were almost overhead and bombs could be expected within ten minutes. This system of warning saved many civilian lives.

Another important use of the net was to find lost aircraft. If a pilot were lost, he could call his control station and ask for assistance. A quick call to the Chinese radio net headquarters generally would provide information that gave us the plane's location.

In late June, 1942, I was at the Kunming AVG radio station talking with our operator, Bob King. He had a call from the leader of a flight of P-40s coming in from India. They were lost and needed help. I called the Chinese net and asked if they had any report of aircraft activity. They told me that the only report was one of heavy engine noise, twenty minutes old, about 100 miles northeast of Kunming. The pilot reported that he was flying over a railroad. There was a railroad line that went in a northwesterly direction from us, and it was apparent that the flight had missed the Kunming airfield and was heading in the wrong direction. Bob King told them to turn around and follow the railroad tracks. They did and landed safely.

The Chinese net also was an excellent communications and intelligence system. It assisted and directed aid to pilots who had crashed, sometimes behind the Japanese lines. It located wrecked Japanese planes and provided other information that was most helpful to the government. The air raid warning net in Yunnan was the most efficient of the Chinese system. The area was divided into twenty kilometer squares. The goal was to have a reporting station in each square.

The inner net around Kunming was the first to be established. Four Chinese net control stations equipped with radio transmitters and receivers were established about forty kilometers from Kunming. Each of these stations had eight outlying telephone reporting points located in one of the twenty kilometer squares. This net covering an area of about sixty kilometers around Kunming was established by 1940 before the AVG came to China.

This inner net had its four sub-control stations at Kunyang, Lotze, Iliyang and Sunming. These stations reported to their control station in Kunming. There were two other major net control stations in Yunnan Province, one at Yunnanyi and the other at Chanyi. Aircraft information from a primary reporting point would be reported to a sub-control station and then relayed to the major net control station of the area. However, these nets were interlocking. Both the sub-stations and the major net control stations guarded each other's radio frequencies. Information could then flow in several directions, and sometimes warning of Japanese activity in the Yunnanyi sector would reach our headquarters at Kunming through the NCS (Net Control Station) at Chanyi before the Yunnanyi NCS reported it.

Yunnan was one of the most backward provinces of China. It has many mountains, rivers and lakes. It is a high land with the plateau at Kunming over 6,000 feet above sea level. Most of the roads in the interior were designed for foot traffic and impassable for trucks or automobiles. There were no telephone or telegraph lines. Therefore, the Chinese reporting stations in most of this rugged country were equipped with radio receivers and transmitters. The small towns and villages in this area had no electric power. Gasoline was very expensive and would have had to be carried in cans to the out-of-the-way locations.

These stations produced their electric power with hand-crank generators. Some luckier stations had the generator attached to a bicycle so that the soldiers assigned to this task could sit down and keep the generator spinning with their leg muscles. Obviously they did not keep the generator and radio operating very long. When they opened the net in the morning about dawn, they would power up and report in to their net control station. Any messages to the operators on duty would be sent at this time. They would then sign off and not go back on the air unless they observed aircraft activity. The net control stations would of course guard their frequency all day, generally using a battery powered receiver to save fuel.

These outlying Chinese reporting stations were staffed with one radio operator, one radio mechanic and two soldiers to act as guards. The operators and mechanics received training at a school in Kunming that was attached to the Chinese Air Force Cadet School. The caliber of the Chinese radio operators and mechanics whom I saw was excellent. Most of the operators were young high school graduates, and their code speed was above twenty-five words a minute. Most of those attached to the AVG had taken some English in high school but had little ability in conversation. The technical requirements for the radio operators and mechanics at the reporting stations were not high, since the equipment was fairly simple, and a fast code speed was not needed as messages were short and made up mostly of numbers. Honesty and dependability were very important plus the fortitude to wait for long hours doing nothing but looking and listening for aircraft.

Some of the Chinese operators had escaped from the Japanese occupation on the east coast and had impressive credentials. I knew of one man who had been a wireless operator on several steamships and had an excellent knowledge of world radio communications. He was put to work as an instructor in the school for radio

Radioman Alex (Mickey) Mihalko with a small friend at Kunming. Mickey was the radio operator at our net control station and highly competent. He came to the AVG from the Navy.

operators in Kunming. By our standards the pay of the Chinese personnel was incredibly low. When inflation began to erode even this small pay, the government furnished all employees with a monthly allowance in rice to help them subsist.

Transmission from the basic net reporting stations was in International Morse Code; they did not have the facilities for voice transmission. This presents an obvious problem, for Chinese is not written in a phonetic alphabet. It has many thousands of characters, each standing for one word. One must know about three thousand characters to read a newspaper. Therefore, the Chinese developed a five number code with each number standing for a Chinese character. Usage of this code was time consuming and cumbersome. In actual practice in the net many words were used repeatedly, and the code numbers were often remembered without access to the book. The stations were furnished with a rather short extract from the code book which covered the vocabulary needed to make sighting reports.

The Chinese also developed a phonetic alphabet that used the Morse code. For example the English letter E is sent in Morse by one "dot." In Chinese the E sound means the number one and is written as a horizontal line. A Chinese operator would write this as a vertical line like our L meaning the sound E in Chinese. The Japanese had a phonetic alphabet and used it to transmit news and propaganda from Tokyo daily. I used to copy it while stationed at Chanyi for practice to improve my code speed. I could identify it since Japanese has many K sounds.

The location of the reporting stations depended upon the terrain. High ground or hilltops offered the best observation posts. However, they had to be close to a village for basic food, water supplies and housing. High, lonely mountain tops were not very practical, and such locations were only used when a station had to cover a wider area due to its strategic location or the lack of other stations in the "squares" of the net.

The Chinese observers were not well trained in aircraft identification, but neither were many of the AVG. They often reported "heavy engine noise" when the sky was overcast or when they could hear planes that were out of sight. We received reports such as "ten two-engined Japanese bombers." They soon were able to identify the P-40s and other common American aircraft. Sometimes we would get estimates of the altitude but not always. Since the Japanese were prone to fly at the same altitudes, the absence of such a report was not a major problem.

The equipment at the reporting stations was not standard. The radios or transceivers, small generators and other parts were mostly purchased in Hong Kong and smuggled into eastern China. They were assembled in Kunming by the Chinese under the direction of John Williams, an ex-army radioman who had come to China in 1939 as an instructor in the Chinese Air Force Cadet School. He had known General Chennault in the American Army Air Corps and had come to China when offered a job by Chennault. Williams was later the communications officer of the American Volunteer Group.

The Chinese spotters at the outlying stations were visited at least once a month by a representative from their headquarters to bring their monthly pay, supplies and mail. However, most mail to these radiomen would be delivered by the Chinese Post Office, since its service was excellent and cheap (although sometimes slow) and covered most of Free China. It also operated behind the Japanese lines.

In order to use effectively the air raid warning net information, it had to be relayed to AVG headquarters and our pilots in the air. For this purpose the AVG radio stations were established. We generally had around thirteen stations in operation. When we lost Burma, the men and equipment were transferred to the eastern China fields. The AVG stations were located near the Chinese net control and sub-control stations. Except for the stations at Kunyang and Lotze, there were good airfields at the AVG radio sites.

The AVG radiomen were given the title of "Station Master" which translates in Chinese to something like "base commander." This was done deliberately to give us "face" in a situation where we might be the only American stationed at a field. We were not given a military title, for we might be outranked by officers of the Chinese Air Force. In actual practice the cooperation of all the Chinese officers was excellent. I was never given any orders by the Chinese, and I gave no orders to any of them. If there was a minor problem, we would discuss it and come to a mutual decision. Discipline of the Chinese airmen and soldiers was completely in the hands of their own officers.

This is a typical AVG receiving station. A map of Yunnan divided into reporting squares is on the wall. Al Kaelin is talking to radioman Sanger.

AVG radio receiver station after it had been taken over by American Air Corps personnel.

Radioman E. O. Bonham in front of the temple at Yunnan-Yi that housed the AVG radio station.

The AVG radio station at Chanyi, where I was stationed from February to June, 1942, was one of the best locations in our radio net. Chanyi was a major Chinese air raid warning net control station site and one of the most efficient in the system. There was a good hostel, equipped for 200 Americans and operated by the War Area Service Corps, or WASC, the Chinese organization that housed and fed the AVG and later the many thousands of Americans of the Air Force from 1942 through 1945. Chanyi also had a 5,000 foot gravel runway. While I was stationed there, I was the only American at the field. Later it was used extensively by the Fourteenth Air Force.

To assure that the radio stationmaster would receive all warning reports, the AVG receiving equipment at Chanyi was located in a small two-room building that also housed a sub-control station and relay point in the Chinese net. This station was manned by one very cheerful Chinese telephone operator named Chang whose English vocabulary was mostly "okay." He had six telephones that connected with the local net control center, the next large town to the north, Pingyi, the local switchboard, and a local sub-net of reporting telephone stations.

All of the reports of enemy activity came from this operator. He would call "jing bow" (air raid). I would answer, "Suh moh de fong?"(where?). His answer

AVG radioman Carson Roberts with an Army sergeant assigned to his station. Carson stayed with the American Army Air Corps as a second lieutenant and later went to flying school and became a pilot. He flew a C-47 to Kunming in 1943 and we had a short visit. He was killed later that year in the Mediterranean theater.

The temple at Kunyang that housed the AVG radio station. I was stationed here for about a week in early 1942.

This is the RCA TE-134-B transmitter used by the AVG radio stations, shown here with the army personnel that replaced the AVG. It was an excellent transmitter with a remote control unit that could dial any one of four frequencies.

John Williams, head of AVG communications, with his dachshund pups. He gave one of the males to Chennault who named it Joe-dog. It was Chennault's constant companion for many years (I have had several dachshunds over the years).

would be the name of a Chinese town or village which would be meaningless to me. We had on the wall of the station a large map of Yunnan on which was superimposed a grid of twenty kilometer squares. The squares at the top of the grid were identified with English letters, A, B, C, etc. The vertical side of the grid were identified with numbers. We would then search for the village or town, assisted by an interpreter if one were present. When the site was found, I could then identify it, for example, as sector L-22. I would then call our net control station BG-8 in Kunming and report "one Japanese plane in sector L-22." I quickly learned the Chinese technical terms for "heavy engine noise," "airplane" and the "numbers."

Japanese planes generally came from Hanoi, and the first report from the net often was "heavy engine noise." The next report often would be more specific, giving the number of planes and the number of plane engines.

The AVG used one frequency, 6,048 kilocycles, for all radio stations. All P-40s transmitted and received on this frequency. General Chennault had a receiver tuned to our net in his office, and the pilots on the field in their "ready room" on the airfields listened to our reports. The result was that everyone who needed to know was informed of Japanese activity at the earliest possible moment. Our planes in the air had the latest reports without delay.

The transmitter used by the AVG stations was a 400-watt, two-channel, RCA TE-134-B with a remote control unit that could be used to dial up to four frequen-

R. M. Smith and Marlin (Bud) Hubler at Cheng-Yi. Hubler later went to flying school and was a major at the end of the war. He died of a heart attack at our reunion at Ojai, California, on July 1, 1977.

Hubler and Kenner in front of the hostel at Chang-Yi. They were on their way up the Burma Road to Chungking.

AVG radioman A. A. Miller with an Army sergeant at his receiver station. Miller remained in China with the Army Air Force and was discharged in 1945. I met him again in 1947 in Los Angeles where he was working on a degree in accounting from the University of Southern California. We had served together in the 20th Pursuit Group at Hamilton Field, California.

cies. It was a good transmitter that was seldom out of order. At Chanyi it was located about one-half mile from the receiving station together with a 5,000 watt gasoline-powered generator and a battery charger. This equipment was located in a small padlocked building. Outside the door was a switch with two buttons, one for "ON" and one for "OFF." A Yunnanese guard was always on duty in front of this building. A direct telephone line was installed, linking the transmitter site to the receiver building. The instruments at each end were the old army field telephones with a hand crank in a leather case. When I wanted the engine started, I would ring the guard and tell him, "Kai gee gee" (start the engine). He would then press the "ON" button, and I would have power to transmit and power for the two radio receivers and lights. Most of the day I guarded the frequency with a battery-powered receiver to save gasoline.

Occasionally I would receive a long coded message from Kunming. This would be in Morse code, and we used another frequency in the 4,000 kilocycle range to receive and transmit. During the reception of such a message I would still guard our voice frequency.

The code we used for messages was a simple one, all numbers. Each letter of the alphabet was represented by two or more two digit numbers. Letters of high frequency such as T and E could be coded by using any one of five different numbers. This code was difficult for the enemy to break, and I doubt that they ever did. The base code was changed frequently.

When I was assigned to Chanyi, I discovered that I was to report the local weather daily or on demand. For this we had a code that reported ten different weather conditions, such as wind direction, type of clouds, rainfall, etc. Each classification had up to ten types, each indicated by a number. There were ten types of clouds listed, each identified by a number from one to ten. I had never heard of some of these clouds. I had read of cumulus clouds in various novels, and I had an idea of the meaning of some of the others. I never reported that we had any cirrostratus clouds at Chanyi.

Each of our three fighter squadrons had communication chiefs whose primary responsibility was to maintain the radios in the P-40s. Louis Wyatt was in charge of communications in the First Squadron, the Adam and Eves. Mickey Mihalko of the Second Squadron, the Panda Bears, was decorated by the RAF for heroism in Rangoon. Charles Francisco was communications chief of the Third Squadron, or Hell's Angels. While their primary responsibility was not that of a net control station master, they often acted as comptroller at the Burma fields, furnishing our pilots with the latest air raid warning information.

There was no warning net in Burma comparable to that in China with an observer in most of the twenty kilometer "squares." However, a warning system was organized by the British, using local telephone and telegraph lines. This helped, of course, but the results were spotty. Our squadrons could not be sure that they would

Radioman Bill Sykes and R. M. Smith in Burma. Bill was very proud of the fact that his great-grandfather was an admiral in the British navy. He went to flying school and was killed in an accident in August, 1943.

be warned of a Japanese attack. As Japanese ground troops neared Rangoon, it collapsed completely. As we withdrew from Burma, the lack of enemy intelligence was to prove costly. The attacks on Loiwing were often with little or no warning.

During our retreat in the battle of Burma, Ed Lussier and Bob King operated their radio station out of a truck, keeping just ahead of the Japanese. They maintained contact with our planes in the air as well as with Kunming. It was our only communications link with the AVG headquarters. At the AVG station at Loiwing, Harvey Cross and Roger Shreffler did yeoman service under hectic conditions. They also transferred their equipment to a truck in the days of the final battles.

All of the radio stationmasters worked at least a twelve-hour day, seven days a week. At my station at Chanyi I welcomed enemy activity, for it was interesting and exciting and relieved the boredom. I was luckier than many stations, as I was on the main Burma Road leading from Kunming to Chungking and the eastern Chinese provinces, and often had visitors. Bob Lindstedt at Lotze and R. L. Richardson at Kunyang had no air fields at their stations and were not on a main highway so guests were rare. Quite often their major companionship was with local missionaries, who always were friendly and invited them to good home-cooked meals. A local chief of the Maotze, the hill tribes, offered one radioman the choice of one of six young girls for companionship. He told me he had to decide between the girl, and the friendship and food of a local man-and-wife missionary team. He declined the chief's offer.

Morgan Vaux at Yunnanyi relieved his boredom by writing the most horrible poetry I had ever heard. It dealt mostly with the methods the Chinese used in fertilizing their fields. He would often come on the air in the morning and read us "the poem for the day." Ralph Sasser, when he was stationed at Mungtze, liked to discuss his sex life in incredible detail over the air and "in the clear." I used to roar with laughter at his stories, remembering that General Chennault had a receiver in his office and that the pilots on the field would be listening with some interest.

Arvo Miller at Paoshan became very friendly with the local missionaries of the China Inland Mission and gave up smoking and drinking. At Kunming our net control station leader Ed (Boogie) Baughman, was in the center of much activity and probably the busiest of us all on a daily basis. Bill Sykes at Chungking found it much more peaceful when he was transferred there from his Burma duties.

In April, 1942, General James Doolittle made his famous raid on Japan. The twenty-five B-25s were to have landed in China in order to become a part of the air force under General Chennault. It would have given us the bombers that we so urgently needed. However, every plane was lost. Fortunately most of the pilots and crew were rescued by the Chinese. If the AVG had installed a homing beacon in one of the eastern Chinese fields, we could have saved most of these bombers.

John Williams on the left and radioman Ernie Bonham, top right, at the time of the transfer of the AVG radio station at Yunnan-Yi to the American Air Corps.

I asked General Doolittle about this when he attended one of the AVG Association reunions at Ojai some years ago. He told me that the American military leaders did not want to tell General Chennault about the raid, since he was so close to the Chinese and they feared that too many people would learn of the proposed action. If many people had known, there might have been leaks to the Japanese. He also told me that they had sent an army C-47 loaded with homing beacons and other communications equipment from the United States to China to be used in guiding the B-25s to the Chinese fields. This plane was lost in an accident en route.

Much credit must go to the Chinese officers and men who organized, manned and supplied the basic air raid warning net. The leaders were skilled and intelligent, and the ground observers patient and dependable. Without them our mission would have been impossible. Later in the war General Chennault published a newsletter for the net personnel to let them know how their work was helping the defeat of Japan. Chennault also obtained observer's wings from the United States which were distributed to the aircraft spotters. Never were wings so well earned.

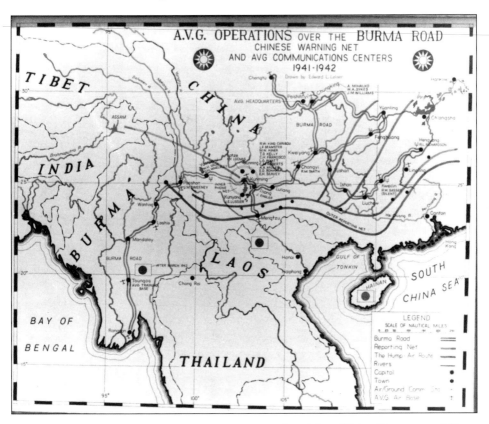

The AVG communications net in China. This map was in the exhibit of Flying Tiger memorabilia at the San Diego Aerospace Museum. The museum burned some years ago and the AVG section is being replaced in the new museum.

4

The AVG After July 4, 1942—The War Years

July 4, 1942, was to have been induction day for the American Volunteer Group. We were all supposed to enter the United States Army Air Corps. The American authorities had wanted to absorb the group earlier, but General Chennault had postponed it as long as he could. Only five pilots and thirty-three ground personnel agreed to join the military services. Tom Trumble, General Chennault's secretary, agreed to stay on as a civilian. This amounted to about fifteen percent of the 253 members of the AVG who received honorable discharges from the Chinese Air Force. This figure includes twenty-three killed and four POWs.

Why were we not all drafted into the American services? There were two main reasons. First, Chennault would not have permitted it. He felt that if we wanted to return to the United States, we had earned that right. Secondly, it was not legally possible. We were members of the Chinese Air Force on foreign soil and not under the jurisdiction of the American government. General Bissel, the commander of the U.S. Air Force troops in India, and his staff threatened us with being drafted as privates in the infantry when we reached the United States. This threat had an adverse effect on the AVG.

Most of the American Volunteer Group did not volunteer, for we felt lost, forgotten and discouraged. Only a few supplies had trickled into China. The few old P-40s that were operational were held together with makeshift repairs and were dangerous to fly. Only a few C-47 transport planes were flying the Hump from India. China was a forgotten theater surrounded by Japanese except for the impassable Tibetan border and the vast northern deserts adjoining Siberia. Our victories had brought us fame in the newspapers and magazines of the United States but had not changed the fact that the major war was being fought in Europe. In China the future looked bleak.

Three Flying Tiger pilots were prisoners of war. Charles D. Mott was captured in Thailand on January 8, 1942. Lewis S. Bishop went down on May 17, 1942, and William McGarry spent the war in a Siamese prison. Joe Alsop, the columnist and our supply officer, was captured in Hong Kong and sent home in a diplomatic exchange.

Eighteen of the AVG pilots, while refusing induction into the Army Air Corps, joined CNAC, the China National Aviation Corporation, a civilian airline owned by Pan-American and the Chinese government. This airline pioneered the famous Hump route that later in 1944 and 1945 reached a volume of almost 1,000 transport planes a day bringing supplies to China from India. Five ground men also worked for CNAC: Dr. Lewis J. Richards, crew chief Frank Losonsky, and three radiomen, Bob King, Robert Shreffler and Loy Seamster. The pay was good, but the job was dangerous. Three AVG pilots were killed while flying this route: Einar Mickelson at Paoshan on February 20, 1944, Allen Wright at Suifi (Ipin) on December 10, 1943, and John Dean on November 17, 1942.

The American Volunteer Group had lost twenty-two pilots and one ground man, including John Petach, Jr., and Arnold Shamblin, who were killed in action on July 10, 1942, after volunteering for two week's extra duty with the new China Air Task Force. While we lost only four pilots in actual aerial combat with the Japanese, the others were lost in bombing missions and accidents. The pilot loss was thirty percent of all pilots honorably discharged.

Before we left China in July, 1942, we were each given a letter from the Air Service Command to the Air Corps Ferry Command authorizing us air transportation to the United States. A few of the early arrivals in Karachi, India, actually did get to fly back to the States. However, after an altercation in a bar, the commanding general ordered that no AVG would be permitted to fly to America. For several weeks about 150 of us hung around Karachi looking for a way to go home. Finally, passage was arranged for us on the *USS Mariposa*, a ship of the American President Lines that had just brought several thousand troops to India. We were charged $150 for third class passage or $600 for first class. Most of us opted for the cheaper rate and slept in the hospital area of the ship in comfortable double bunks. The food was excellent. The Mariposa sailed from Karachi on July 27 to Bombay, where it stayed until August 6. After thirty-five days at sea, with one stop at Cape Town, South Africa, we landed in New York in mid-September, 1942.

When we debarked, we were informed by the customs people that we had to register for the draft within three days. I registered in New York as living in California. This apparently slowed the paper work, for I was not notified to appear for induction until many months later after I had re-enlisted in the air corps.

When I arrived at my home in Southern California, I found a letter waiting for me from the War Department in Washington. It stated that "the Commanding General, Army Air Forces, appreciates your excellent work with the AVG." It was suggested that I report to the nearest Air Force station and re-enlist. I was promised a higher grade if I would do so. In October I visited March Field Air Force Base and re-enlisted as a technical sergeant and was assigned to a field at Glendale, California. A new fighter squadron was being formed, the 337th, and I was appointed its communications chief. In February, 1943, I was sent to the Officer Candidate School at Miami Beach. After graduation I was assigned to the Army Airways Communications System in Texas.

I reported to Major Jess R. Guthrie, who had just been ordered to command the AACS group covering the airfields in northern Assam in India and China. When he found out that I had been in China with the AVG, he asked, "Do you want to go back?" I said yes and a month later flew with him from Miami back to India in a C-87 transport plane by way of Puerto Rico, Brazil, Ascension Island, Africa and Karachi. It took us eight days to make the trip.

We spent one night in Khartoum, Anglo-Egyptian Sudan, where the British were still talking about how the AVG pilots had swindled the local merchants in early 1942. Our pilots had flown to Africa to pick up new P-40Es for the American Volunteer Group. These pilots had purchased many souvenirs, using Chinese paper currency. Chinese money was printed in English on one side and on the other in Chinese. (A Chinese dollar was worth about two cents U.S.) Our pilots had told the merchants that this was American money and that the Chinese writing was the American Indian script. Since the local merchants had a reputation for high prices and double dealing, the British considered it a rare joke.

When I arrived in Kunming, I went to General Chennault's headquarters to pay a courtesy call. I found Doreen Davis (now Reynolds), who had visited my radio station at Chanyi after escaping from Hong Kong, working as his secretary. I had an enjoyable talk with the General about the AVG days.

The AACS station in Kunming was small with only a few men assigned. One year later, with the heavy increase in air transport from India, I had over 250 officers and men in my communications detachment, almost as many as had been in the American Volunteer Group. Later I was appointed the first commanding officer of the 159th AACS Squadron with headquarters in Chungking. There were seventeen radio stations in this squadron, all located in northeastern China, with four of them reporting weather from Chinese Turkestan.

Walt Dolan returned to China as a crew chief in a fighter squadron. We spent a happy day together in Chengtu with a bottle of locally made whiskey "brewed under the direction of American experts." Some pilots from Kentucky had shown the Chinese how to set up a mountain still.

Eight of the AVG ground crew went to flying school after their return to the United States and became pilots. Radioman Carson Roberts flew a C-47 over the Hump to China in 1943 and looked me up in Kunming. A few months later he was killed in North Africa. Another radioman, Bill Sykes, also graduated from flying school and was killed in an accident at Williams Field, Arizona, in August, 1943. I remember that Bill was so proud of his great-grandfather, who was an admiral in the British navy.

The third radioman who completed pilot's training was R. L. Richardson. He had better luck and retired as a colonel and command pilot from the Air Force. Armorer Donald L. Rodewald was also a command pilot who made the Air Force his career. When he returned to China as a fighter pilot, it was too late to see any action. However, he shot down one MIG in Korea. He is an honorary member of the Fighter Aces Association. An accident left him paralyzed from the waist down, but this does not prevent him from driving his own car or flying his own plane. In 1984 he was the first paraplegic to fly solo around the world. He was the Flying Tiger Pilot Award winner in 1987.

Armorer Robert P. Rasmussen became a bomber pilot and was killed in Action in North Africa in 1943. Marlin R. Hubler, an operations clerk in the AVG, went to flying school and was discharged as a major at the end of the war. E.B. McClure, a crew chief, joined the Navy and took flight training. He retired as a lt. commander. Jesse R. Crookshanks, who retired from the Air Force, was a pilot shot down over Germany while flying a bomber. He was held as a prisoner of war until hostilities ended.

Armorer Charles N. Baisden went to flying school but washed out. He later was a gunner on Robert T. Smith's bomber, Barbie III, in India and Burma. In late 1944 Dick Rossi was flying for CNAC on the Hump between Assam and China. He had heard that Robert T. Smith was stationed at the Air Commando base in Halicandi in northeast India and decided to pay him a visit. R.T. was a friendly fellow and offered Rossi the best hospitality of the base, including a flight in his B-25 as co-pilot. Although Dick was a civilian, he accepted. R.T. Smith led a flight of three B-25s and eight P-51s on a photo reconnaissance and bombing mission to the Japanese fields in Burma. Rossi had his camera along and was busy taking motion pictures through the ship's clear nose. After photographing the Japanese fields, they started for home while looking for a "target of opportunity." They found a busy railroad yard and dropped five hundred pound bombs.

There was no Japanese opposition. Charlie Baisden, without warning, decided to fire the seventy-five millimeter cannon. There was a horrible noise, and the Plexiglas nose of the B-25 flew off. At first they thought they had been hit by Japanese ground fire. It was extremely cold in the cockpit; Rossi had a jacket on, but R.T. was in his shirt sleeves. They made it back to the base and while landing, the B-25 following them saw an unexploded 500 pound bomb dangling from Smith's plane. It was too late to take any evasive action. The bomb hit the ground, bounced and landed in a nearby ditch. The firing mechanism had been damaged on impact, and the bomb did not explode. Rossi and Smith never did figure out why the nose of the B-25 flew off. Dick thanked R.T. and Charlie for an interesting day and went back to flying the Hump. The great quotes from that escapade were furnished by Lydia Rossi, Dick's wife:

R.T. Smith: "And to think I volunteered for this mission!"

Dick Rossi: "I'm a civilian on vacation! What am I doing here?"

A total of fifteen of the AVG were killed in action or by accidents in the years between July, 1942, and the end of the war in 1945. These included the three ground men who became pilots and the three AVG pilots killed while working for CNAC. Five of these deaths occurred in China: Boatner Carney in October, 1942, and Roy G. Hoffman, both at Chanyi in late 1942; Frank Scheil, Jr., on December 22, 1943; George B. McMillan on January 7, 1944; and William N. Reed, in January, 1944, both at Henyang.

Parachute rigger Burton L. Hooker was killed in Honduras in an accident in November, 1943. My friend Jim Musick died at DeWitt Army Hospital in October, 1944. Harry R. Bolster, Robert Brouk and Eugene Durall all died in Florida accidents in late 1942 or early 1943.

Most of the members of the American Volunteer Group came from the Army Air Force, the Navy or the Marines. Therefore it was natural for them to return to the military services. Some of the AVG who remained in China with the China Task Force were given naval commissions or ratings. At least thirty-five of our group who survived remained in their respective services until retirement. Besides General Chennault, two AVG pilots retired with star rank: General James H. Howard, who also won the Congressional Medal of Honor in Europe, and Major General Charles R. Bond. Tex Hill, a colonel in the Air Force, was later a brigadier general in the Texas National Guard.

Many of the members of the American Volunteer Group carried the practical knowledge they had learned under Chennault to the Army and Navy Air Forces. Our pilots were able to teach others a tactical approach that was exceedingly efficient. But, best of all, they brought a feeling of esprit de corps—a knowledge that Americans could win under difficult circumstances and against long odds. We were welcomed back to the armed services and given opportunities and further challenges. Many had to work a little harder, for we had a reputation to maintain.

5

The AVG After World War II

The members of the American Volunteer Group were children of the Great Depression. In the 1930s jobs were hard to find. Many young men enlisted in the Army or Navy or, if they had at least two years of college, applied for pilot training at the service schools. The Army and Navy had waiting lists of applicants trying to enlist for $21 a month. A high school diploma was required, and a strict physical examination had to be passed. In addition, an intelligence test was used to further weed out the potential enlistees. Since the Army and Navy Air Forces were particularly desirable, these branches of the service were able to select the best men from the long waiting lists. In the Army Air Force when World War II started, many master sergeants were promoted directly to captain. It was not unusual for enlisted men to hold reserve commissions.

Therefore it is not surprising that after the war so many of the AVG were successful in either the military or civilian life. Of those who stayed in the service, three became generals and five retired as colonels or naval captains. Twenty-three of our pilots were airline captains. Many entered the business world and were very successful. Three Flying Tigers started restaurants, including George Lum, who owns an excellent Chinese-American establishment in Flushing, New York.

AVG ace Charles Older attended law school after the war and became a Los Angeles Superior Court judge. He attained national attention as the cool-headed judge in the notorious Manson trial. Double-ace Ken Jernstedt retired as a state senator in the state of Oregon.

Robert Gallagher, who was a nurse with the AVG, went to medical school and earned his M.D. AVG pilot Carl Brown also became a doctor of medicine and has a large practice in Southern California. Dr. Lewis J. Richards, our genial and efficient doctor with the AVG, was in practice well into his 80s and discussed weight control with some of the AVG members in a rather pointed fashion. Our AVG dentist, Dr. Everett W. Bruce, practiced in Knoxville, Tennessee. Emma J. Foster, an AVG nurse, married pilot John E. Petach, Jr., in China before the dissolving of the American Volunteer Group. John volunteered for an additional two weeks of service in July, 1942, and was killed in action at Nanchang on July 10. Mrs. Petach returned home on the *Mariposa*, and her daughter Joan was born in the United States. Emma, better known as "Red," is now married to a former CNAC pilot, Fletcher Hanks, and is active in Maryland Republican politics. She was president of the Maryland Women's Republican Association and is a vice president of the Flying Tigers Association. Supply clerk Leo A. Beaupre also went back to school after the war to become a doctor. He is practicing in St. Petersburg, Florida.

The Flying Tiger Line was the world's largest all-cargo airline. When it was organized in 1945, there were several hundred other small, similar operations started by World War II pilots using surplus aircraft. One CAB official said, "Every time I blow my nose, another idiot airline is born." It was a new industry with no guidelines. Competition was keen, and few companies survived.

The Flying Tiger Line was founded by Robert W. Prescott, AVG ace. Eleven World War II pilots and ground crew joined Prescott in raising $89,000, which was matched by Sam Mosher of the Signal Oil Company. I remember receiving a letter from Bob Prescott asking me to invest. I refused and lost an opportunity that would have been very profitable. American Volunteer Group members who did invest and/or worked for the airline were William E. Bartling, J. R.(Dick) Rossi, R.P.

When the Flying Tiger Line started operations they relied heavily on the Douglas C-47, the cargo version of the famed DC-3.

The Curtiss C-46 that flew the Hump joined the Flying Tiger Line fleet in 1949.

(Duke) Headman, Clifford G. Groh, Jack Cornelius, C.J. Rosbert, Tom Haywood, Link Laughlin, R.J. Raine and Bob King. When Bill Bartling died in 1979, he was retired vice president in charge of operations. The first name of the fledgling outfit was the National Skyway Freight Corporation. It was changed to the Flying Tiger Line when the members of the American Volunteer Group Association approved the use of the Flying Tiger name.

It took much courage to enter the air freight business at the close of World War II when about 2,000 eager pilots were establishing some kind of an air company. The early years of the Flying Tiger Line were difficult, and the company was often on the verge of bankruptcy. Later it had over 4,000 employees and its stock was traded on the New York Stock Exchange.

The Hungry Tiger Restaurant chain was founded by two of the original American Volunteer Group and two friends. Robert W. Prescott and John (Dick) Rossi were joined by Len Kimball, public relations director of the Flying Tiger Lines, and Doug Gamble, an attorney. These restaurants featured excellent fresh seafood flown in by the Flying Tiger Line. They had expanded to forty-two locations in four western states before they sold to W.R. Grace Co.

Two of the AVG who joined without service background have become well known in their fields. Joe Alsop, our supply officer, became a noted columnist.

Gerhard Neumann, an AVG mechanic who escaped from Hitler's Germany, headed General Electric's jet aircraft engine group. He wrote a book called "Herman the German."

The spirit of adventure was evident in the lives of many of the American Volunteer Group after the war. Some became private pilots. Mel Kemph was engaged in crop dusting. Irving Stolet, Bob Locke and Robert J. Neal all became civilian pilots. Crew chief Irving Gove took his whole family on a cruise from Europe to Florida in a sailing craft. Jesse Crookshanks was a crash inspector for the Federal Aviation Administration.

A number of Flying Tigers have written books. General Chennault's *Way Of A Fighter* is an excellent story of his life and the challenges that he met. Our chaplain, Paul Frillmann, collaborated with Graham Peck to write *China, The Remembered Life*, which tells his story in the American Volunteer Group and his later experiences in China in front-line intelligence activities. After Paul's experience as our padre, he never went back to preaching again.

Don Whelpley, AVG weatherman, wrote *Weather, Water and Boating* in 1961. It is a small-craft sailor's guide to the weather and became a classic. Olga Greenlaw published her story during World War II as *The Lady And The Tigers*. Greg Boyington has written two books, one of which became the basis of the television series *Baa*

A Flying Tiger Line C-54 used to supply the American Occupation Forces in Japan. Its speed was 210 miles per hour.

Accepting Flying Tiger Line's first B-747 Freight Master in Wichita, Kansas. Tiger Board Chairman Wayne M. Hoffman and President Robert W. Prescott, right, receive the key to the aircraft from E. H. Boullioun, president of Boeing. Boeing employees painted the tiger shark face on the nose to recall the colorful founding of the all-cargo airline by Prescott and eleven other members of the AVG.

Baa Black Sheep. General James H. Howard wrote *Roar Of The Tiger.* Pilot C. Joseph Rosbert produced a different book, *Adventure Story Cookbook.* He asked members of the AVG for recipes and various adventures. Chuck Baisden carried on with the book, *Flying Tiger To Air Commando. A Flying Tigers Diary* is the story by Major General Charles R. Bond, Jr. R.T. Smith's book, *Tale Of A Tiger*, has gone through several editions. *Flying Tiger - A Crew Chief's Story*, was written by Frank S. Losonsky. Erik Shilling's book, *Destiny*, sub-titled *A Flying Tiger's Rendezvous With Fate*, is a most interesting story of his adventures.

For many years the American Volunteer Group has held its reunions in the beautiful Ojai Valley in southern California. Over the years we have become better acquainted, and the friendships that began in the jungles of Burma and mountains of China have developed into very close relationships for many of us. One wife called us "a band of brothers." Until the FAA put a stop to it, the Flying Tiger Line flew the group members, their families and friends, free from all over the United States and a few foreign countries to our reunion site. As the Flying Tiger Line

From Budds to Boeings. The Budd Conestoga was the first freighter in 1945. The Boeing 747 is shown below.

Generalissimo Chiang Kai-shek and Madame Chiang with General Chennault in 1942. Note the Chinese star on Chennault's hat.

Jane Mansfield and Chennault at an AVG reunion in 1957. It was the last reunion that he attended.

handles mostly cargo, the accommodations were often sparse, but the price was right.

Since so many of our members joined CNAC during the war, their organization also met with us for the reunions. This is where Fletcher Hanks, CNAC pilot, met "Red" Petach, and began a courtship that led to a happy marriage. Until it was discontinued in 1991, the AVG gave an award every other year to one who had made an outstanding contribution to flying and aerospace. Winners of the Flying Tiger Pilot Trophy include Neil A. Armstrong, the first man on the moon, General Chennault, Major General Charles R. Bond, Jr., and Robert W. Prescott.

We have lost track of some of the original members of the American Volunteer Group, In the list of all those who received honorable discharges from the Chinese Air Force at the end of this book, their names are followed by "no address." Any information about these men will be appreciated by the secretary of the AVG Association, Lt. Col. Donald Rodewald, P.O. Box 906, Lake City, Colorado 81235.

Of course, all of the original Flying Tigers did not become rich and famous. Most of us had careers that showed qualities of steady dependability and competence (I myself enjoyed a career in banking). A few had a battle with alcoholism, but one joined AA and learned to enjoy life without drinking.

It is difficult to accurately describe the AVG. My story is from the point of view of a radioman and from a diary that was written at the time of our battles. We have been written of as heroes, mercenaries, soldiers of fortune, patriots, adventurers and idealists. *Time* magazine wrote a nasty article about us emphasizing our rowdiness and pay scale. Of course we were mercenaries—we were paid well. We were also a government-sponsored operation. But compared to the cost of other groups, our results made the price the Chinese government paid very cheap. Some were patriots and idealists, but most of us liked to make money. We loved adventure but knew it often meant outside toilets, jungle heat, snakes, bugs and poor food. Whatever the American Volunteer Group has been called, it was unquestionably unique in its historical impact as the deadliest group of fighter pilots ever to blaze the skies in defense of freedom. The record of the American Volunteer Group has never been surpassed.

SECRETARY OF THE AIR FORCE
WASHINGTON

The President of the United States takes pleasure in presenting the

PRESIDENTIAL UNIT CITATION
to
THE AMERICAN VOLUNTEER GROUP
FLYING TIGERS
for service as set forth in the following citation:

The American Volunteer Group Flying Tigers distinguished itself by extraordinary heroism in connection with military operations against opposing armed forces in South China and Southeast Asia from 7 December 1941 to 18 July 1942. During this period, members of the American Volunteer Group displayed exceptional valor in compiling an unparalleled combat record. Although never manned with more than 70 trained pilots nor equipped with more than 49 combat ready P-40 fighter aircraft, this volunteer unit conducted aggressive counter-air, air defense and close air support operations against numerically superior enemy forces occasionally 20 times larger, members of the American Volunteer Group destroyed some 650 enemy aircraft while suffering minimal losses. Their extraordinary performance in the face of seemingly overwhelming odds was a major factor in defeating the enemy invasion of South China. The professionalism, dedication to duty, and extraordinary heroism demonstrated by the members of the American Volunteer Group Flying Tigers are in keeping with the finest traditions of the military service and reflect the highest credit upon themselves and the Armed Forces of the United States.

FOR THE PRESIDENT

Donald B. Rice

Donald B. Rice

Finally, in 1991 the United States Government admitted that the AVG was an official covert operation and gave a Presidential Unit Citation to the American Volunteer Group—the original Flying Tigers. Also, medals are pending for all members.

Appendix A:
American Volunteer Group—Chinese Air Force Honorably Discharged Members, November 1996

C. BRYANT ADAIR, Staff
Deceased, 24 February 1992

FRANK W. ADKINS, Pilot
Deceased Dec. 23, 1996, Palm Beach, FL

JAMES L. ALLARD, Auto Mechanic
Deceased, 26 August 1978

JOSEPH W. ALSOP, JR., Staff
(P.O.W. Exchanged)
Deceased, 28 August 1989

FRANK A. ANDERSEN (JACOBSON)
Crew Chief

JOHN D. ARMSTRONG, Pilot
Deceased, 8 September 1941, Burma

PETER W. ATKINSON, Pilot
Deceased, 25 October 1941, Burma

G.R. BAILEY, Crew Chief

CHARLES N. BAISDEN, Armorer

WILLIAM E. BARTLING, Pilot
Deceased, 19 November 1979

EDMOND C. BAUGHMAN, Communications
Deceased, 1954

DR. LEO A. BEAUPRE, Supply Clerk
Deceased, 20 March 1995

DONALD BELL, Supply Clerk
(no address)

MORTON W. BENT, Op. Clerk

LEWIS S. BISHOP, Vice Sqdn. Leader
(P.O.W. – 3 years)
Deceased, 1 November 1987

JOHN E. BLACKBURN III, Pilot
Deceased, 28 April 1942, Kunming

WILLIAM J. BLACKBURN, Crew Chief

HAROLD J. BLACKWELL, Crew Chief
(no address)

HARRY R. BOLSTER, Pilot
Deceased, 10 October 1944
Elgin Field, FL

CHARLES R. BOND
Vice Squadron Leader

E.O. BONHAM, Communications

JAMES E. BRADY, Supply Clerk
(no address)

KENNETH V. BREEDON, Clerk
(no address)

GEORGE BRICE, Crew Chief
Deceased, 8 December 1982

J. GILPIN BRIGHT, Pilot
Deceased, 22 July 1973

ROBERT R. BROUK, Pilot
Deceased, 19 December 1942
Orlando, FL

CARL K. BROWN, M.D., Pilot

EVERETT W. BRUCE, D.D.S.,
Dental Surgeon Dental Surgeon
Deceased, 27 February 1987

CARL F. BUGLER, Adm. Clerk
Deceased, 27 February 1987

GEORGE T. BURGARD, Pilot
Deceased, 5 October 1978

MICHAEL R. CALLAN, Crew Chief

BOATNER R. CARNEY, Staff
Deceased, October 1942, Chanyi

JOHN B. CARTER, Line Chief
Deceased, 25 October 1974

HERBERT R.CAVANAH, Pilot
Deceased, 14 January 1988

MELVIN E. CEDER, Staff
(no address)

CHARLES CHANEY, Crew Chief
Deceased, 1979

CLAIRE LEE CHENNAULT, C.O.
Deceased, 27 August 1958

KEITH J. CHRISTENSEN, Armorer

ALLEN B. CHRISTMAN, Pilot
Deceased, 23 January 1942,
Rangoon

L.P. CLOUTHIER, Op. Clerk

THOMAS J. COLE, JR., Pilot
Deceased, 30 January 1942
Moulmein, Thailand

LEON P. COLQUETTE, Crew Chief
Deceased, 26 September 1992

EDWIN S. CONANT, Pilot
Deceased, 1965, San Diego

JACK CORNELIUS, Crew Chief

CHARLES D. CRIBBS, Medical Dept.
(no address)

JOHN S. CROFT, Pilot
Deceased, 3 February 1968, Penns.

JESSE R. CROOKSHANKS
Crew Chief
Deceased, 12 February 1991

HARVEY G. CROSS, Communications
Deceased, 19 December 1988

JAMES D. CROSS, Pilot
Deceased, 25 February 1989

GEORGE F. CURRAN, Crew Chief

ALBERT D. CUSHING, Op. Clerk
Deceased, 1984

OTTO W. DAUBE, Crew Chief

W.H.S. DAVIS, Staff
Deceased, August 1977, Australia

JOHN J. DEAN, Pilot
Deceased, 17 November 1942
Hump Crash

WALTER J. DOLAN, Crew Chief
Deceased, 20 January 1983

JOHN T. DONOVAN, Pilot
Deceased, 12 May 1942, Hanoi

FRANCIS DORAN, Clerk

CARL E. DORRIS, Adm. Clerk
Deceased, 25 December 1980

PARKER S. DUPOUY, Vice Sqdn. Ldr.
Deceased, 16 May 1994

EUGENE G. DURALL, Clerk
Deceased, 28 August 1943,
Miami Beach, FL

CHARLES R. ENGLE, Crew Chief
Deceased, 24 August 1993

JOHN ENGLER, Communications
(no address)

RICHARD J. ERNST, Communications
(no address)

JOHN W. FARRELL, Pilot
Deceased, March 1969, Kansas City

JOHN E. FAUTH, Crew Chief
Deceased, 22 March 1942, Magwue

WILLIAM H. FISH, JR., Pilot
Deceased, October 1987

EDWIN L. FOBES, Clerk

BEN C. FOSHEE, Pilot
Deceased, 4 May 1942, Paoshan

HARRY E. FOX, Line Chief
Deceased, 1964, Mineral Wells, TX

CHARLES H. FRANCISCO,
Communications
Deceased, 1970 San Diego

PAUL W. FRILLMAN, Chaplain
Deceased, 19 August 1972

ALLEN W. FRITZKE, Armorer

E.F. GALLAGHER, Crew Chief

ROBERT GALLAGHER, Nurse
Deceased, 28 November 1971

JOSEPH GASDICK, Crew Chief
Deceased, 8 February 1990

CHUN YUEN GEE, Engineering
(no address)

THOMAS C. GENTRY, M.D.
Chief Surgeon
Deceased, 7 December 1971

HENRY M. GESELBRACHT, Pilot
Deceased, 15 July 1969
Burbank CA

HENRY G. GILBERT, JR., Pilot
Deceased, 23 December 1941, Rangoon

LLOYD L. GORHAM, Crew Chief
Deceased, 18 May 1955

IRVING P. COVE, Crew Chief

EDGAR T. GOYETTE, Pilot

P.J. GREENE, Pilot

HARVEY K. GREENLAW, Staff Officer
Deceased, 10 January 1983

OLGA S. GREENLAW, Clerk
Deceased 1993

CLIFFORD G. GROH, Pilot
Deceased, 10 November 1979

LESTER J. HALL, Pilot
Deceased

MAX C. HAMMER, Pilot
Deceased, 22 September 1941,
Rangoon

EMMA JANE HANKS (FOSTER-
PETACH),
Nurse

JASPER J. HARRINGTON, Line Chief
Deceased, 17 August 1996

DAVID H. HARRIS, Staff

EDWARD J. HARRIS, JR., Adm. Clerk
Deceased, 10 Jan. 1981

THOMAS C. HAYWOOD, JR., Pilot
Deceased, 1979

ROBERT P. HEDMAN, Pilot
Deceased, 24 May 1995

J.J. HENNESSY, Pilot
Deceased, 28 March 1991

THOMAS M. HENSON, Medical Dept.
Deceased, 1978

DAVID LEE HILL, Pilot
Sqadron Leader

FRED S. HODGES, Pilot
Deceased, October 1976

LOUIS HOFFMAN, Pilot, Staff
Deceased, 26 January 1942
Rangoon

ROY G. HOFFMAN, Staff
Deceased, late 1942, Chanyi

BURTON L. HOOKER, JR.
Parachute Rigger
Deceased, 27 November 1943
Rangoon

JAMES H. HOWARD, Pilot, Sq. Ldr.
Deceased, 18 March 1995

DANIEL J. HOYLE, JR., Adm. Clerk
(no address)

MARLIN R. HUBLER, Op. Clerk
Deceased, 1 July 1977, Ojai, CA

LYNN A. HURST, Pilot
Deceased, 21 September 1974

EDWIN A. JANSKI, Propeller Mech

KEN A. JERNSTEDT, Pilot

THOMAS A. JONES, Vice Sqdn. Ldr.
Deceased, 16 May 1942, Kunming

JOE T. JORDAN, Clerk
Deceased, 1965, Los Angeles, CA

WALTER C. JOURDAN, JR., Weather
(no address)

ALBERT V. KAELIN, Clerk

ROBERT B. KEETON, Pilot

DANIEL H. KELLER, Crew Chief
(no address)

THOMAS D. KELLY, Telephone Lineman
Deceased, July 1983

MERLYN D. KEMPH, Crew Chief

CHARLES D. KENNER, Crew Chief
Deceased

GEORGE B. KEPKA, Crew Chief

MELVIN W. KINER, Telephone Lineman
Deceased, 26 February 1991

ROBERT J. KING, Communications
Deceased, 14 September 1984

STEPHEN KUSTAY, Armorer
Deceased, 15 June 1991

MATTHEW W. KUYKENDALL, Pilot
Deceased, 22 August 1974,
Austin TX

LAWRENCE W. KWONG, Staff
Deceased, 1977

C.H. LAUGHLIN, Pilot
Deceased, 25 March 1995

FRANK L. LAWLOR, Pilot
Deceased, 1973

BOB LAYHER, Pilot

CHARLES C. LEAGHTY, Parachute
Rigger
(no address)

JOSEPH S. LEE, Flight Surgeon
Deceased, 1 May 1995

PAK ON LEE, Engineering
Deceased May 1, 1995

EDWARD J. LEIBOLT, Pilot
Deceased, 26 February 1942
Rangoon

ROBERT K. LINDSTEDT, Communications
Deceased, 29 October 1990

JACK R. LINTON, Armorer
(no address)

E.W. LOANE, Pilot
Deceased, 17 January 1978

ROBERT L. LITTLE, Pilot
Deceased, 22 May 1942, Salween River

ROBERT P. LOCKE, JR.
Propeller Mechanic

ELTON V. LOOMIS, Communications
Deceased

FRANK S. LOSONSKY, Crew Chief

GEORGE L. LUM, Engineering

JOSEPH E. LUSSIER, Communications
(no address)

LACY F. MANGLEBURG, Pilot
Deceased, 24 December 1941
Lotien Shwangpo

NEIL G. MARTIN, Pilot
Deceased, 23 December 1941
Rangoon

GAIL E. McCALLISTER, Crew Chief

E.B. McCLURE, Crew Chief

WILLIAM D. McGARRY, Pilot
(P.O.W. – 3 years)
Deceased, 6 April 1990

S.L. McHENRY, Clerk – Engineering

EUGENE R. McKINNEY, Armorer

GEORGE G. McMILLAN, Vice Sq. Ldr.
Deceased, 7 Jan. 1942, Hengyang

KENNETH T. MERRITT, Pilot
Deceased, 7 January 1942, Rangoon

EINER I. MICKELSON, Pilot
Deceased, 20 February 1944
CNAC Flt. #75, Paoshan

ALEX MIHALKO, Communications
Deceased, 1970, Banner Elk, NC

ARVOLD A. MILLER, Communications
(no address)

CHARLES V. MISENHEIMER, Crew Chf.
Deceased, 4 February 1991

KENNETH R. MOSS, Weather
(no address)

ROBERT C. MOSS, Pilot
Deceased, 9 October 1993

CHARLES D. MOTT, Pilot
(P.O.W. – 3 years)

WILLARD L. MUSGROVE, Crew Chief

JAMES H. MUSICK, Armorer
Deceased, 5 October 1944
Dewitt Army Hospital

ROBERT J. NEAL, Armorer
Deceased, 11 August 1981

ROBERT H. NEALE, Pilot, Sq. Leader
Deceased, 29 November 1994

GERHARD NEUMANN, Mechanic

JOHN V. NEWKIRK, Pilot, Sq. Leader
Deceased, 24 March 1942
Chiang Mai, Thailand

CHARLES H. OLDER, Pilot

ARVID E. OLSON, Pilot, Sq.
Ldr. Deceased, 16 May 1974

HENRY L. OLSON, Crew Chief

HAROLD L. OSBORNE, Crew Chief
(no address)

E.F. OVEREND, Pilot
Deceased, 6 August 1971
JOHN L. OVERLEY, Crew Chief

PRESTON B. PAULL, Crew Chief
Deceased, 7 March 1985

GEORGE LEE PAXTON, Pilot
Deceased, 17 September 1979

JOSEPH N. PEEDEN, Crew Chief Deceased, 26 April 1974

R.C. PERET, Line Chief
Deceased, 29 November 1980

P.J. PERRY, Armorer
Deceased Jan. 19, 1997

JOHN E. PETACH, JR., Pilot
Deceased, 10 July 1942, Nan Cheng

JOSEPH H. PIETSKER, Photographer
Deceased, 18 January 1949
Birmingham, AL

HERB PISTOLE, Armorer

KEE JEUNG PON, Engineering
(no address)

JOSEPH A. POSHEFKO, Armorer

ROBERT W. PRESCOTT, Pilot
Deceased, 3 March 1978

DR. SAM PREVO, Flight Surgeon
Deceased, 1964

ALBERT E. PROBST, JR., Pilot
Deceased, October 1981

CARL QUICK, Crew Chief
Deceased, September 1996

Robert J. RAINE, Pilot

ROBERT P. RASMUSSEN, Crew Chief
Deceased, 31 May 1944
Mediterranean Theatre

Edward F. RECTOR
Vice Squadron Leader

WILLIAM N. REED, Pilot
Deceased, January 1944, Henyang

JAMES E. REGIS, Photographer
Deceased

STANLEY J. REGIS, Crew Chief

DOREEN REYNOLDS, Secretary
Deceased, 17 June 1986

DR. LEWIS J. RICHARDS, Flt. Surg.
Deceased, 30 October 1992

ROLLAND L. RICHARDSON
Communications

FREEMAN I. RICKETTS, Pilot
Deceased, 31 August 1977

WAYNE RICKS, Propeller Mechanic
Deceased, 13 January 1990

CLARENCE W. RIFFER, Armorer
Deceased, 15 January 1991

CARSON M. ROBERTS, Communications
Deceased, 1943
Mediterranean Theatre

DONALD L. RODEWALD, Armorer

ROBERT W. ROGERS, Crew Chief
Deceased, 4 January 1986

CAMILLE J. ROSBERT, Pilot

JOHN R. ROSSI, Pilot

JOHN M. RUMEN, Armorer

ROBERT J. SANDELL, Pilot, Sq. Ldr.
Deceased, 7 February 1942, Rangoon

RALPH W. SASSER,
Communications, Deceased

CHARLES W. SAWYER, Pilot
Deceased, 8 May 1978

W.E. SCHAPER, Group Engineering
Chief

FRANK SCHEIL, JR., Vice Sq. Ldr.
Deceased, 22 December 1943, China

RALPH F. SCHILLER, Armorer
(no address)

LEO J. SCHRAMM, Crew Chief

LOY F. SEAMSTER, Communications
Deceased, 22 May 1986

EDWARD H. SEAVEY, Op. Clerk
(no address)

WILFRED R. SEIPLE, Crew Chief
Deceased, 13 January 1992

ARNOLD W. SHAMBLIM, Pilot
Missing in action, 10 July 1942

VAN SHAPARD, JR., Pilot
Deceased, 27 June 1976

JOHN E. SHAW, Medical Dept.
(no address)

GEORGE LEO WING SHEE, Engineering
Deceased, 5 April 1968

MILAN SHIELDS, Propeller Mechan.

E.E. SHILLING, Pilot

ROGER SHREFFLER, Communications

CURTIS E. SMITH, JR., Adjutant, Pilot, Deceased, 1960

ROBERT A. SMITH, Crew Chief

ROBERT H. SMITH, Pilot

ROBERT M. SMITH, Communications

ROBERT T. SMITH, Pilot
Deceased, 24 August 1995

JO B. STEWART SHURRETTE, Ch.Nurse

ED L. STILES, Crew Chief

IRVING J. STOLET, Crew Chief

WILLIAM L. SUTHERLAND, Auto Mech.
Deceased, 1965

FRANK W. SCHWARTZ, Pilot
Deceased, 24 April 1942,
Poona, India

JOSEPH H. SWEENEY, Communications
Deceased, 29 January 1975

WILLIAM A. SYKES, Communications
Deceased, August 1943
Williams Field, AZ

JULIAN E. TERRY, Clerk
Deceased, 1 August 1971
Indianapolis, IN

W.H. TOWERY
Mess Supervisor

TOM TRUMBLE, Sec. to Chennault

CHESTER A. TULEY, Crew Chief
(no address)

GEORGE TYRRELL, Crew Chief

JOHN J. UEBELE, Crew Chief
Deceased, 10 August 1989

FRANK E. VAN TIMMEREN, Line Chief

MORGAN H. VAUX, Communications

HUGH J. VIVERETTE, Medical Dept.

EARL F. WAGNER, Armorer
Deceased, 1 July 1974

M. WAKEFIELD, JR., Crew Chief
(no address)

GEORGE WALTERS, Clerk
Deceased, 30 March 1991

DON WHELPLEY, Weather
Deceased, 10 October 1988

ELOISE WHITWER, Steno-Typist
Deceased, 16 February 1973

JOHN M. WILLIAMS, Communications
Deceased, 3 January 1993

CLIFFORD H. WILSON, Auto Mechanic
Deceased, 8 January 1946

H.C. WIRTA, Armorer

FRITZ E. WOLF, Pilot

MELVIN H.WOODWARD, Crew Chief

ALLEN M. WRIGHT, Pilot
Deceased, 10 December 1943
CNAC #83, Suifu, China

PETER WRIGHT, Pilot

LEM FONG WU, Engineering
Deceased, July 1971

LOUIS G. WYATT, Communications
Deceased

HAROLD G. WYLIE, Clerk

FRANCIS T.F. YEE, Engineering

JOHN P. YOUNG, Clerk, Engineering

Appendix B:
American Volunteer Group
Confirmed Victories

Pilot	Number of Planes	Pilot	Number of Planes
A		Brown, C. K.	.25
Adkins F. W.	1		
		Burgard, G. T.	10.75
B			
Bacon, N. R.	3.50	**C**	
		Cole, T. J.	1
Bartelt, R. R.	7		
		Cross, J. D.	.25
Bartling, W. E.	7.25		
		D	
Bishop, L. S.	5.20	Dean. J. J.	3.25
Blackburn, J. E.	2	Donovan, J. T.	4
Bolster, H. R.	2	Dupouy, P. S.	3.50
Bond, C. R.	8.75	**F**	
		Farrell, J. W.	1
Boyington, G.	3.50		
		G	
Bright, J. G.	6	Geselbracht, H.M.	1.50
Brouk, R. R.	3.50	Greene, P. J.	2

Pilot	Number of Planes	Pilot	Number of Planes
Groh, C. G.	2	**M**	
		Merritt, K. T.	1
Gunvordahl, R. N.	1		
		Mickelson, E. I.	.25
H			
Hasty, R. L.	1	Moss, R. C.	4
Haywood, T. C.	5.25	Mott, C. D.	2
Hedman, R. P.	4.83	McGarry, W. D.	10.25
Hill, D. L.	12.25	McMillan, G. B.	4.25
Hodges, F. S.	1	**N**	
		Neale, R. H.	15.50
Hoffman, L.	.25		
		Newkirk, J. V.	10.50
Howard, J. H.	6.33		
		O	
J		Older, C. H.	10.25
Jernstedt, K. A.	10.50		
		Olson, A. E.	1
Jones, T. A.	4		
		Overend, E. G.	5.83
K			
Keeton, R. B.	2.50	**P**	
		Petach, J. E.	4
Kuykendall, M. W.	1		
		Prescott, R. W.	5.25
L			
Laughlin, C. H.	5.20	**R**	
		Raines, R. J.	3.20
Lawlor, F. L.	8.50		
		Rector, E. G.	6.50
Layher, R.	.83		
		Reed, W. N.	10.50
Leibolt, E. J.	.25		
		Ricketts, F. L.	1.20
Little, R. L.	10.50		

Pilot	Number of Planes
Rosbert, C. J.	4.50
Rossi, J. R.	6.25
Sandell, R. J.	5.25
S	
Sawyer, C. W.	2.25
Schiel, F.	7
Shapard, V.	1
Shilling, E. E.	.75
Smith, R. H.	5.20
Smith, R. T.	8.66
W	
Wolf, F. E.	2.25
Wright, P.	3.65
Total	**297**

NOTE: Published lists of victories of AVG aces differ; some contain obvious errors. Since this list originated with George L. Paxton, AVG finance officer, and our pilots received five hundred dollars for each confirmed victory, it is probably the most accurate. Many planes shot down were never confirmed, for they fell into the bay near Rangoon or into Burmese jungles. Including planes destroyed on the ground, the total destroyed was probably 650.

Appendix C:
H81-A-2 Airplanes Used by the
American Volunteer Group

A.V.G. No.	SQDN No.	Pilot & Remarks	Curtis Seq. No.
P-8101	92	Hedman	626
P-8102			627
P-8103	3	Rossi Abandoned in Rangoon.	628
P-8104			631
P-8105	6	Dean	632
P-8106			633
P-8107		Crashed in training. Schiel bailed out OK.	637
P-8108	37	Ricketts	639
P-8109	68	Older	640
P-8110	42	Fish	641
P-8111			646
P-8112		Head-on collision on Sept. 8 with P-8117. Armstrong killed.	647
P-8113	2		652
P-8114		Engine transferred to P-8127	653
P-8115	69	Bishop	660
P-8116			661
P-8117		See P-8112 Bright bailed out OK.	667
P-8118	70	Olson	668
P-8119	71	Overend, Smith, C.E.	674
P-8120	43	Keeton	675
P-8121	88	Jernstedt	681
P-8122			682
P-8123	36	Rector	688
P-8124			689

Curtis Ser. No.	Date Delv. To Toungoo	Test Flown	Delivery Pilot
15337	11-28	11-26	Glover
15338	8-18	8-12	Olson
15339	8-18	7-15	Cook
15423	10-9	10-6	Greene
15424	8-18	8-8	Atkinson
15425	8-21	7-8	Moss
15430	9-1	8-21	Petach
15431	8-7	7-23	Glover
15432	8-20	8-1	Walroth
15433	9-5	9-2	Howard
15438	10-27	10-25	Olson
15439	8-20	7-24	Martin
15444	8-20	6-29	Little
15445	8-26	7-19	Newkirk
15452	8-22	8-16	Dupouy
15453	10-29	10-14	Wright
15459	8-29	7-12	Probst
15460	8-22	8-4	Neale
15466	8-28	8-21	Swindle
15467	9-6	9-6	Mangleburg
15473	10-31	8-13	Merritt
15474	8-22	8-22	Sawyer
15480	8-22	8-8	Geselbracht
15481	8-3	8-1	Glover

A.V.G. No.	SQDN No.	Pilot & Remarks	Curtis Seq. No.
P-8125	1	Atkinson was killed in this plane.	695
P-8126		Spun in by Hammer on Sept. 22	696
P-8127	47 14	Petach was killed in this plane. Had engine from P-8114.	702
P-8128	54	Christman	703
P-8129			709
P-8130			710
P-8131	35		716
P-8132	15		717
P-8133	49	Schwartz	722
P-8134	48	Hill	723
P-8135	79	Hedman	729
P-8136	40	Cole	730
P-8137			736
P-8138	57	Howard	742
P-8139	99	Olson	749
P-8140			756
P-8141			763
P-8142	41	Paxton, Merritt, Bacon	770
P-8143	10	Farrell	777
P-8144			784
P-8145			790
P-8146			792
P-8147	52	Shilling, Martin	794
P-8148	98	McMillan	796
P-8149	58		796
P-8150			800
P-8151	33		802
P-8152	56	Bright	804
P-8153		Shilling, Photo plane. Had only 2 guns.	806
P-8154	97	Foshee	808
P-8155			810
P-8156	46	Lawlor	812

Curtis Ser. No.	Date Delv. To Toungoo	Test Flown	Delivery Pilot
15487	8-28	7-25	Merritt
15488	8-9	7-31	Glover
15494	10-4	10-4	Jones
15495	11-7	11-4	Older
15501	10-27	10-25	Newkirk
15502	10-4	10-3	Smith
15508	8-30	8-27	Armstrong
15509	10-10	10-8	Christman
15514	10-9	10-7	Smith
15515	10-4	10-1	Bright
15521	10-4	10-3	Schiel
15522	8-28	7-16	Rushton
15828	10-2	10-1	Wolf
15834	11-16	11-15	Bright
15841	11-22	11-13	Cole
15848	11-16	11-15	Wright
15855	11-16	11-16	Hodges
15862	9-22	9-22	Newkirk
15869	10-7	10-2	Leibolt
15876	11-12	11-11	Farrell
15882	11-16	11-14	Hedman
15884	9-20	9-18	Neale
15886	10-15	10-6	McMillan
15888	11-19	11-18	McMillan
15890	11-19	11-18	Smith
15892	11-10	11-8	Hastey
15894	11-17	11-16	Little
15896	11-16	11-14	Greene
15898	11-21	11-20	Paxton
15900	11-17	11-14	Liebolt
15902	10-1	9-30	Shilling
15904	10-2	10-1	Bacon

A.V.G. No.	SQDN No.	Pilot & Remarks	Curtis Seq. No.
P-8157		Lost overboard in loading. Rescued and used for spare parts.	
P-8158			816
P-8159			818
P-8160			819
P-8161	59	Bacon	821
P-8162	94	Haywood	823
P-8163			824
P-8164	11	Sandell	826
P-8165	45	Bartelt, Moss	828
P-8166			829
P-8167			831
P-8168	85	Brouk	833
P-8169			834
P-8170	53,13	Layher	836
P-8171	50	Ricketts	838
P-8172			839
P-8173	77	Smith, R.T.	841
P-8174			843
P-8175			845
P-8176			847
P-8177	38	Geselbracht	848
P-8178			850
P-8179			852
P-8180			853
P-8181	51	Cole	855
P-8182	21	Boyington	857
P-8183	83	Hodges	858
P-8184	44	Wright	860
P-8185			862
P-8186	75	Reed	863
P-8187			865
P-8188			867
P-8189			869
P-8190	16		870
P-8191	90	Dupouy	871
P-8192			872
P-8193			873

Curtis Ser. No.	Date Delv. To Toungoo	Test Flown	Delivery Pilot
15908	10-7	9-22	Hill
15910	10-4	10-3	McMillan
15911	11-5	10-28	Hill
15913	11-19	11-17	Hastey
15915	11-14	11-13	Bartling
15916	11-10	11-10	Merritt
15918	11-16	11-15	Howard
15920	11-9	11-8	Criz
15921	11-14	11-13	Geselbracht
15923	11-12	11-11	Haywood
15925	11-12	11-12	Mott
15926	9-6	9-4	Geselbracht
15928	10-17	10-16	Sawyer
15930	10-10	10-18	Rector
15931	9-5	9-3	Bright
15933	9-15	8-15	Criz
15935	8-30	8-20	Howard
15937	9-11	9-3	Hodges
15939	9-18	9-13	Hastey
15940	9-11	9-6	Swindle
15942	8-27	8-25	Brouk
15944	10-21	9-12	Jones
15945	9-15	9-19	Sawyer
15947	10-11	9-10	Mott
15949	10-15	9-17	Walroth
15950	10-10	9-18	Hedman
15952	9-15	9-12	Mott
15954	10-17	10-15	Reed
15955	9-12	9-11	Kelleher
15957	9-12	9-11	Martin
15959	9-1	8-23	Bacon
15961	9-1	8-23	Sandell
15962	9-4	9-3	Shilling
15963	11-7	11-5	Jernstedt
15964	9-5	9-3	Wright
15965	10-10	10-9	Kuykendall

A.V.G. No.	SQDN No.	Pilot & Remarks	Curtis Seq. No.
P-8194		Sawyer	874
P-8195	84	Greene	875
P-8196	34	Newkirk	876
P-8197	18	Kuykendall	877
P-8198			878
P-8199			879
P-8200	39	Moss	880

Notes on A.V.G. plane numbers:

1.Squadron numbers were often changed due to transfers to another squadron or after an accident to keep numbers in sequence order.

For example, the Second Squadron on December 17, 1941, listed its planes numbering from 34 through 59, with no missing numbers, although there had been a number of accidents that totally destroyed at least eight planes in this squadron.

2.The First Squadron was assigned plane numbers from 1 through 33, the Second Squadron from 34 through 67, and the Third Squadron from 68 through 99. Replacement planes (P-40Es) were assigned numbers above 100.

3.The American Volunteer Group received as replacements at least 33 P-40Es numbered from 101 through 134. Twelve of these planes were flown to China by our own pilots from Africa. The Tenth Air Force received 19 P-40Es from the A.V.G. after July 4, 1942.

4.Not all pilots were assigned planes, since there were generally more pilots than aircraft. The assignment of a plane to a pilot did not guarantee him its exclusive use.

Curtis Ser. No.	Date Delv. To Toungoo	Test Flown	Delivery Pilot
15966	11-25	11-24	Wolf
15967	10-15	9-15	Mangleburg
15968	9-8	9-8	Glover
15969	11-11	11-10	Hodges
15970	10-17	9-15	McGarry
15971	10-15	9-12	Schiel
15972	9-2	9-2	Wolf

Selected Bibliography

Archibald, Joseph. "Commander Of The Flying Tigers: Claire Lee Chennault". New York: Messner, 1966

Ayling, Keith. "Old Leatherface Of The Flying Tigers". New York: Bobbs-Merrill, 1945.

Belden, Jack. "Retreat With Stilwell". Garden City. N.Y.: Blue Ribbon Books, 1944.

Boyington, Gregory. "Baa Baa Black Sheep". New York: G. P. Putnam's Sons, 1958.

Boyington, Gregory. "Tonya". New York: Bobbs-Merrill, 1960. A novel based on the author's American Volunteer Group experience.

Caiden, Martin. "The Ragged, Rugged Warriors". New York: E. P. Dutton, 1966. Several chapters are concerned with the AVG or the China Air Task Force and Claire Lee Chennault.

Chennault, Anna. "Chennault And The Flying Tigers". New York: Paul S. Erickson, 1963.

Chennault, Anna. "The Education of Anna". New York: Times Books, 1980.

Chennault, Anna. "A Thousand Springs: The Biography Of A Marriage". New York: Paul S. Erickson, 1962.

Chennault, Claire Lee. "The Role Of Defensive Pursuit". Maxwell Field, Alabama: Air Corps Tactical School, ca. 1933.

Chiang Kai-shek, Madame Mayling Soong Chiang. "We Chinese Women". New York: John Day, 1943. It has the author's speech to the AVG and Chennault's response. It has other speeches also.

Chinese Air Force. "Chinese Air Force Volunteer Group". Taipei, Republic of China: General Headquarters of the Chinese Air Force, no date.

Coe, Douglas. "The Burma Road". New York: Messner, 1946.

Cooke, David. "War Wings: Fighting Planes Of The American And British Forces". New York: McBridge, 1941.

Cooke, David. "War Planes Of The Axis". New York: McBridge, 1942.

Craven, Wesley, and James Cate, editors, "Plans And Early Operations" (The Army Air Force in World War II Series).

Chicago: University of Chicago Press, 1948. This volume and Volumes 4 and 5 contain the official account of the China Air Task Force and the Fourteenth Air Force.

Craven, Wesley, and James Cate, editors. "The Pacific: Guadalcanal To Saipan". Chicago: University of Chicago Press, 1950.

Craven, Wesley, and James Cate, editors. "The Pacific: Matterhorn To Nagasaki". Chicago: University of Chicago Press, 1953.

Craven, Wesley, and James Cate, editors. "Services Around The World". Chicago: University of Chicago Press, 1958.

Dorn, Frank. "Walkout: With Stilwell In Burma". New York: Crowell, 1971.

Feis, Herbert. "The China Tangle: The American Effort In China From Pearl Harbor To The Marshall Mission". Princeton, N. J.: Princeton University Press, 1953.

Frillman, Paul, and Graham Peck. "China: The Remembered Life".

Boston: Houghton Mifflin, 1968. The AVG chaplain tells his story.

Gallagher, O.D. "Action In The East". Garden City, N.Y.: Doubleday, Doran, 1942. The book has two chapters on the AVG.

Greenlaw, Olga (Bogert Rogers, editor). "The Lady And The Tigers". New York: E. P. Dutton, 1943.

Gurney, Gene. "Five Down And Glory: – History Of American Aces". New York: G. P. Putnam's Sons, 1958.

Hagar, Alice. "Wings For The Dragon". New York: Dodd, Mead, 1945.

Hahn, Emily. "Chiang Kai-shek". New York: Doubleday, 1955.

Haughland, Vern. "The AAF Against Japan". New York: Harper and Row, 1948.

Heiferman, Ron. "Flying Tigers: Chennault Of China". New York: Ballantine Books, 1971.

Hotz, Robert, editor. "Way Of A Fighter: The Memoirs Of Claire Lee Chennault". New York: G. P. Putnam's Sons, 1949.

Hotz, Robert, with assistance of George Paxton, Robert Neale and Parker Dupouy (AVG pilots). "With General Chennault: The Story Of The Flying Tigers". New York: Coward-McCann, 1943.

Kinert, Reed. "America's Fighting Planes". New York: Macmillan, 1943.

Leonard, Royal. "I Flew For China". Garden City, N.Y.: Doubleday,

Doran, 1942. Captain Leonard was Chiang Kai-shek's personal pilot. The book has a chapter on Chennault.

Liang, Chin-Tung. "General Stilwell In China, 1942-44: The Full Story". Jamaica, N.Y.: St. John's University Press, 1972. It has many references to Chennault.

Liu, F.F. "Military History Of Modern China, 1924-1949". Princeton, N.J.: Princeton University Press, 1956.

Loomis, Robert. "Great American Fighter Pilots Of World War II". New York: Random House, 1961.

Loomis, Robert. "The Story Of The U.S. Air Force". New York: Random House, 1959.

Lyall, Gavin, editor. "The War In The Air: the Royal Air Force In World War II". New York: William Morrow, 1968. This book contains an article by Kenneth Hemingway, an RAF pilot, who tells of his first battle over Rangoon, Burma, against the Japanese.

Mitchell, Ruth. "My Brother Bill". New York: Harcourt, Brace, 1953. This is the biography of General William "Billy" Mitchell.

Moser, Don. "China-Burma-India". Alexandria, Virginia: Time-Life Books, 1978.

Nalty, Bernard. "Tigers Over Asia". New York: Elsevier-Dutton, 1978.

Pistole, Larry M. "The Pictorial History Of The Flying Tigers". Orange, VA.: Moss Publications, 1981.

Romanus, Charles, and Riley Sunderland. "Stilwell's Command Problems". Washington, D.C.: Office of the Chief of Military History, Department of the Army, 1956.

Romanus, Charles, and Riley Sunderland. "Stilwell's Mission To China". Washington, D.C.: Office of Military History, Department of the Army, 1953.

Romanus, Charles, and Riley Sunderland. "Time Runs Out In CBI". Washington, D.C.: Office of the Chief of Military History, Department of the Army, 1959.

Rosholt, Malcolm. "Days Of The Ching Pao: A Photographic Record Of The Flying Tigers – Fourteenth Air Force In China In World War II". Amherst, Wisconsin: Rosholt House, 1978.

Rosholt, Malcolm. "Dog Sugar Eight". Amherst, Wisconsin: Rosholt House, 1977. This is a novel about a radioman in China.

Sakai, Saburo, Martin Caidin and Fred Saito. "Samurai!" New York: Dutton, 1957. The book does not mention the AVG, but it gives an excellent background on Japanese pilot training and dedication.

Scott, Jay. "America's War Heroes". Derby, Conn: Monarch Books, 1961. The book is a series of stories on war heroes, including Gregory Boyington telling his AVG and Marine Corps experiences.

Scott, Robert, Jr. "God Is My Co-pilot". New York: Charles Scribner's Sons, 1944. The book has a foreward by Chennault.

Scott, Robert, Jr. "Flying Tiger: Chennault Of China". Garden City, N. Y.: Doubleday, 1959.

Shamburger, Page, and Joe Christy. "The Curtiss Hawks". Kalamazoo, Mich.: Wolverine Press, 1972. Chapter 8 is on AVG planes.

Sims, Edward. "American Aces In Great Fighter Battles Of World War II". New York: Harper and Row, 1958.

Smith, Nicol. "Burma Road". New York: Bobbs-Merrill, 1940.

Spence, Jonathan. "To Change China: Western Advisors In China". Boston: Little, 1969. It has a chapter on Chennault.

Stilwell, Joseph (Theodore White, editor and arranger). "The Stilwell Papers". New York: Sloane, 1948.

Toland, John. "But Not In Shame". New York: Random House, 1961.

Toland, John. "The Flying Tigers". New York: Random House, 1963.

Toliver, Raymond, and Trevor Constable. "Fighter Aces Of The U.S.A". Fallbrook, Ca.: Aero Publishers, 1979. The book lists AVG aces.

Tuchman, Barbara. "Stilwell And The American Experience In China, 1911-1945". New York: Macmillan, 1970. Chennault is the villain and Stilwell the hero in this book.

Walters, Maude Owens. "Combat In The Air". New York: D. Appleton Century Company, 1944. Contains letters from J. Gilpin Bright, AVG ace.

Wedemeyer, Albert. "Wedemeyer Reports". New York: Holt, 1958.

Whelan, Russell. "The Flying Tigers". New York: Viking Press, 1943.

Flying Tiger Pilot Award Winners

1952 - Capt. Russell J. Brown, First American pilot to down a MIG – Korea.
1954 - William B. Bridgeman, Pioneer pilot on the X3.
1956 - George F. Smith, First pilot to survive supersonic bailout.
1957 - A. M. "Tex" Johnson, First pilot to fly the 707.
1958 - Lt. General Claire Lee Chennault.
1959 - Maj. Walter W. Irwin, world speed record in F-104 -1404 MPH.
1962 - Maj. Robert M. White, First pilot to qualify as an astronaut in an airplane—X-15.
1964 - Col. Lee, Chinese Air Force, for distinguished classified mission.
1965 - Col. Robert L. Stephens, Lt. Col. Daniel Andre, pilots of the YF-12A to new world speed and altitude records.
1967 - Maj. Gen. Charles R. Bond, Jr., 35-year career in military aviation from fighter pilot to commanding general.
1969 - Col. Thomas P. Stafford, Apollo 10 Commander.
1971 - William P. Lear, Sr., Aircraft and electronics pioneer.
1973 - Lt. Gen. Samuel C. Phillips, USAF Director, Apollo Manned Lunar Landing Program.
1975 - Neil A. Armstrong, Astronaut, First man on the moon, Commander of Apollo XI, the moon ship.
1977 - Gen. Chas. E. Yeager, USAF, First man to break the sound barrier,and first to fly at twice the speed of sound.
1979 - Robert W. Prescott, Fighter Ace and founder of The Flying Tiger Line.
1981 - Robert A. Hoover, for his distinguished combat record and outstanding skill as an acrobatic and test pilot.
1983 - Gen. James H. Doolittle, USAF. A lifetime of pioneer contributions to aviation progress and innovations.
1985 - Barry M. Goldwater, USAF Gen. and U.S. Senator. Devoted lifetime of service to his country and to military aviation.
1987 - Lt. Col. Donald L. Rodewald, USAF (Ret.) First paraplegic to fly around the world solo in a single engine airplane.
1989 - Richard C. Rutan and Jeana Yeager. Helped develop and build, then crewed the Voyager in the first nonstop and nonrefueled around-the-world flight.
1991 - Paul Poberenzny. Founded the EAA (Experimental Aircraft Association). The EEA's Oshkosh facility is considered the world's finest permanent Fly-In site.
1992 - B. Gen. James H. Howard, USAF MOH. Only fighter pilot in the ETO to receive the Medal Of Honor.
Lt. Gen. John P. "Jack" Flynn. Flew P-51s in Italy. Shot down over Hanoi, badly injured, he spent 5 1/2 years as a POW, including time in the "Hanoi Hilton."

Index

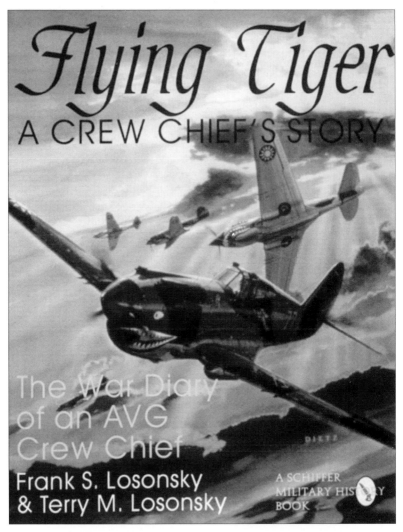

FLYING TIGER: A CREW CHIEF'S STORY - THE WAR DIARY OF AN AVG CREW CHIEF

Frank S. Losonsky & Terry M. Losonsky.

This book is the war diary of a Flying Tiger American Volunteer Group crew chief from the 3rd Pursuit Squadron. *Flying Tiger* will give aviation historians new insights into the days shortly before the Flying Tiger successes in late 1941.
Size: 8 1/2" x 11" 200 photographs
112 pages, hard cover
ISBN: 0-7643-0045-8 $35.00